THE THOMAS RACKETT PAPERS

THE THOMAS RACKETT PAPERS
18TH–19TH CENTURIES

Edited by

H.S.L. DEWAR

Second Edition revised by

ANN SMITH

DORSET RECORD SOCIETY

VOLUME 21

First published 1965
Second edition published 2021 by Dorset Record Society
Dorset History Centre, Bridport Road, Dorchester, Dorset DT1 1XA

General Editor: Dr Mark Forrest

Typeset in ITC New Baskerville by John Chandler,

British Library Cataloguing in Publication Data:
A catalogue record for this book is available from the British Library.

ISBN 978-0-900339-24-0

CONTENTS

LIST OF ILLUSTRATIONS

Front cover: Portrait of Thomas Rackett the younger as a boy by George Romney, 1768.
Back cover: A view of Spetisbury Church by Rev. Thomas Rackett [Hutchins *History of Dorset* 2nd edition, 1796-1815, Vol. III, P. 140]

Front cover image courtesy of Dorset County Museum.
Images 3,4 from RCHM *Dorset* Vol. 3 Central volume, 1970 (Crown copyright).
Images 1,2 and 7 from the Rackett Collection (D-RAC), courtesy of the Dorset History Centre.
Back cover image and images 5, 6, 8, and 9 from Hutchins *History of Dorset* 2nd edition 1796-1815, courtesy of the Dorset History Centre

INTRODUCTION TO THE FIRST EDITION

The Rev. Thomas Rackett, born in 1757, died in 1841, is now chiefly known as an Antiquary, and to a number of Archaeologists and Numismatists as the collector of autonomous and other Greek coins found in the neighbourhood of Spetisbury and Charlton Marshall, where for over 60 years he held the living. It must be mentioned here that this fine collection of coins is in the possession of the Dorset County Museum. Although for decades the origin of the collection was viewed with some scepticism by certain scholars, the coins, together with others in the same category have been accepted by Dr. D.B. Harden, O.B.E., F.S.A., and Dr. J.G. Milne, D. Litt., as authentic Dorset finds[1]. A letter from a clergyman and neighbour of Rackett, now published, throws fresh light on the way in which some of these coins came to Rackett's hand, and will be of interest to any sceptics who may still be with us.

It is the Editor's hope that the publication of the Rackett Papers by the Dorset Record Society will widen and revive interest in, and attention to, the work of this remarkable man. When he was 14, he recited to David Garrick, the Poet and Dramatist, the latter's ode composed for the Shakespearian Jubilee. Unquestionably Romney's splendid portrait of the boy, which is produced here as the frontispiece, shows him in the act of declaiming it. So versatile and accomplished was Rackett in maturity that one can well imagine the Muses all standing round his cradle in his birth-year to decide which of them should secure his talents.

A student of all arts and sciences, in the end he certainly became the master of many. He was taught to draw by Paul Sandby, while the great John Hunter[2] was concerned to interest him in Natural History. He was a good musician, and studied Natural Philosophy, numbering Tiberius Cavallo among his intimates. Even when he was in his eighties he found it possible to take up the study of Conchology and to correspond with the experts of the time.

He Matriculated from University College Oxford in 1773, graduating B.A. in 1777 and M.A. in 1780. It was perhaps the chance influence of Obadiah Walker, a former Master of his College in the late 17th Century, through *Greek and Roman History Illustrated by Coins and Medals*, that caused Rackett to channel his wide interests towards History and its antiquities. Therefore, of the Muses, it was Clio who eventually claimed him and caused the Biographers of modern days to dub him 'Antiquary'. He was a

1 Letter from Rev. J. Cooke of Blandford and Chettle, 10 May 1833
2 John Hunter (1728-1793) was a distinguished surgeon and scientist, who was appointed surgeon at St George's Hospital and was later surgeon to George III. He was elected fellow of the Royal Society in 1767. He put together a large collection of specimens of plants and animals, which he arranged in his house in Leicester Square as a teaching museum.

Fellow of the Royal Society, the Linnean Society and Society of Antiquaries, as well as a Member of the *Société Statistique Universelle*[3] and many other learned bodies. Among his artistic achievements were many fine drawings for John Hutchins' *History of the County of Dorset,* for which General John Bellasis acknowledges indebtedness in the Preface to the 2nd Edition. In these he collaborated with the Chevalier de Barde and his friend Cavallo. The Plates include the Cromlech at Portesham, Cranborne Manor House, Fielding's house at East Stower, and Bearings of Objects seen at Badbury.

In 1781, Rackett married Dorothea, the daughter of the Rev. Thomas Tattershall, Rector of St Paul's, Covent Garden and of Streatham. On his mother's side he was descended from a Huguenot family of merchants named Caillouel, who arrived in England in 1685, and several Caillouel letters written from Boston, New England, have been included herein. Perhaps it was to his mother's side that Rackett owed his passion for collecting both information and objects in the form of documents and letters and bits of paper, that almost amounted to hoarding. We are fortunate indeed that this was so. The Rackett collection of 162 bundles in the Dorset County Record Office, consisting of nearly 1,500 documents, comprises not only letters from such personalities as Mrs Garrick, Dr. W.G. Maton, Physician to Queen Charlotte, Charles Hatchett the Chemist, Sir Richard Colt Hoare, Richard Gough, Mrs Pulteney, John Knowles, biographer of Fuseli, Mrs Siddons, Miss Seward and other prominent persons, but an astonishing assortment of oddments as well. There are Election Manifestoes, notices of performing fleas, an advertisement for a chimney sweep, together with many Genealogical and Heraldic notes, petitions and scientific Memoranda. In sum, these have presented a considerable task of selection, and unavoidably much has been omitted that some members may have found of interest. Those selected have inevitably found their place by being of interest to the Editor who has had to deal with what Professor W.K. Rose of Vassar College, U.S.A., Editor of *The Letters of Wyndham Lewis,* calls '.... the raw material or detritus (depending on your angle) ....'.

During the long years of his incumbency, Rackett led an extremely busy, and consequently happy, life. If his Scientific studies in London and his outdoor pursuits such as riding through half-a-dozen Counties with his learned friends, or digging ancient burial mounds with his daughter Dorothea, took up much time that could have been given to Parish work, he was not the only Parson of this period to delegate duties to a Curate. We have but to take a cross-section of his correspondence to appreciate that he was one of the best examples of the type of country clergy who graced the 18th and early 19th century with their learning and accomplishments.

Rackett's biographers in the *Dictionary of National Biography* and elsewhere[4] have somewhat glossed over the matter, but it is only historically fair to record that his

3 Société Francaise Statistique Universelle. Founded in 1829. It aimed 'to aid the progress of statistics and the development of every branch of human knowledge', which it divided into 'physical and descriptive', 'positive and applied', and 'moral and philosophical' categories.

4 Despite extensive searches, no other biographies of Thomas Rackett have come to light. His obituary appeared in the *Gentleman's Magazine,* April 1841 and others can be found in D-RAC/D/80 and D-RAC/H/141B.

long absences from Spetisbury were eventually brought to public attention by Lord Lansdowne's charges of maladministration brought against him in the House of Lords. That they were ultimately dropped can be attributed to the fact that they were probably due to some six members of his flock joining the Church of Rome. At that time there existed a Convent of Augustine Nuns at Spetisbury.

Rackett was author of *A Description of Otterden Place and Church and of the Archiepiscopal Palace of Charing in the County of Kent*; accompanied by *Genealogical Memoirs of the Family of Wheler*, and *Anecdotes of Some of the Early Experiments in Electricity*, London, 1832. With Dr. W.G. Maton he wrote *An Historical Account of Testaceological Writers*, published in Transactions of the Linnean Society. As was the fashion of his day, he spent some time with such harmless diversions as the setting and solving of riddles and enigmas, as well as composing minor verse. Specimens of both these pastimes have been included here among the Papers. Perhaps the best of all are the many letters addressed to him and to Mrs Rackett and to Dorothea by their numerous friends and relatives.

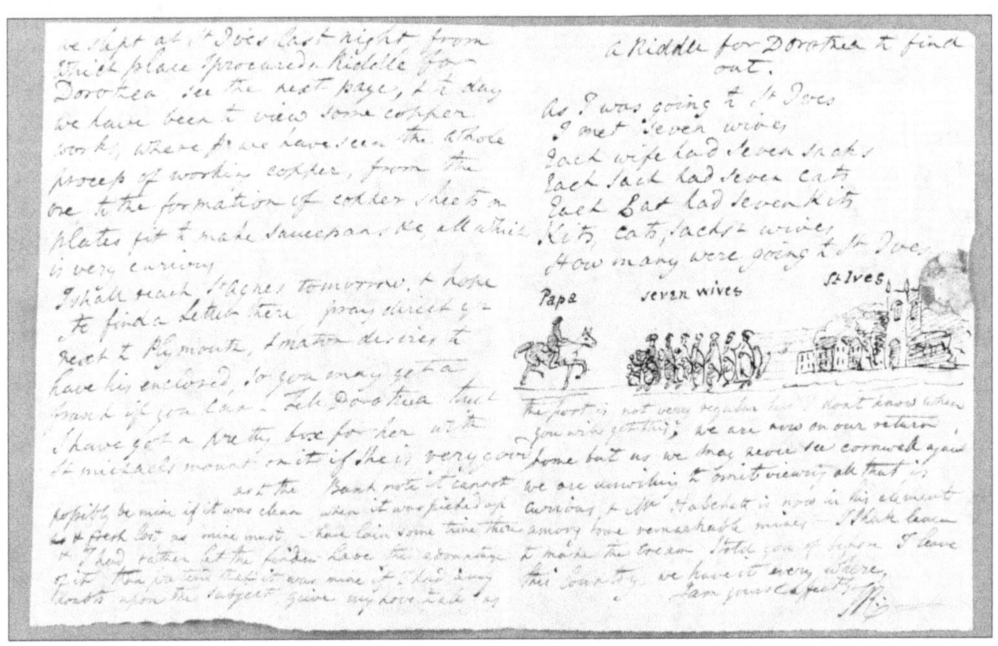
A Riddle for Dorothea to find out.

As I was going to St Ives
I met seven wives
Each wife had seven sacks
Each sack had seven cats
Each cat had seven kits
Kits, cats, sacks & wives
How many were going to St Ives

1 Riddle by Rackett, drawn for his young daughter about 1795 [D-RAC/D/81]

Examples of this correspondence from as far afield as India, Moscow, Nova Scotia and Cape Town have been included. Subjects as disparate as the manufacture of salt, trans-Atlantic agriculture, caverns, dog-stealing, politics and dry rot in His Majesty's ships cannot fail to hold readers' interests, and must often be arresting. Sad to say we have but few examples of letters written by Rackett, but much can be gathered from those he received. In particular, a letter from Thomas King, Paymaster of the 98th Regiment in Canada, published here, portrays vividly a picture of Rackett in his own home, by the fireside, furnished with a glass of substantial port, rubbing his nose, reading and conversing to his wife and daughter, can be recommended as giving us a picture, seen through the nostalgic eye of a protégé, and showing us a very human being as well as a man of scientific attainments.

All the letters and papers have been transcribed as they appear in the originals. In cases where a word is ill-spelt, or there appears to be a grammatical error, the word *sic* has been added in brackets. Where a word or words cannot be read owing to faded ink or other cause, this has been stated. Editorial notes and comments have been kept to a minimum compatible with reasonable clarity. The Editor wishes to record his great appreciation of the kindness of Lt. Col. R.J.N. Solly for permission to publish these papers in the Rackett Collection which have been deposited in the County Record Office in Dorchester. To Miss M. Holmes, M.A., The County Archivist and her staff, he wishes to offer sincere thanks for the trouble taken in looking out the many documents asked for, and for help in deciphering and interpretation. Thanks are also due to Mrs. S.M. Campbell, M.A., and Mr R.N.R. Peers, M.A., A.M.A. for their help.

H.S.L. Dewar

INTRODUCTION TO THE SECOND EDITION

In 1965 Dorset Record Society published its third volume, *The Thomas Rackett Papers*, edited by H.S.L. Dewar. At that time the Society's volumes had card covers which were stapled on and the texts were produced on a manual typewriter. The new edition of Volume 3 has benefitted from the facilities afforded by modern technology. The text has been re-typed which has allowed the silent correction of minor textual errors in the original, the incorporation of Dewar's *errata* into the text, and the introduction of italics for book titles and foreign words. The footnotes have been expanded and more illustrations have been included. The opportunity has been taken to move some letters at the end, presumably included at the last minute by Dewar for their interest, into their proper chronological sequence. Two previously unpublished letters, one from Mary Anning and one mentioning her, have been added for their interest. The most visible difference is that, using modern digital printing, Dorset Record Society is now able to produce this new edition in hardback with an illustrated cover.

Hubert Stephen Lowry Dewar (known as Stephen) was born in 1892 at Doles Lodge, Enham near Andover. He was descended from a line of minor gentry of Scottish origin who settled in Hampshire in the 18th century. From an early age he was interested in archaeology, excavating a barrow in Doles Wood at the age of 13. After Cambridge he went out to India as a tea planter. During the First World War, he served as a lieutenant in the Indian Army Reserve, returning to England in 1926 and settling at Catcott in Somerset. He was involved in a number of important excavations, including the Neolithic timber causeway in the Brue Valley and the Roman Villa at Low Ham. He subsequently wrote, lectured and broadcasted about the archaeology of the area. In 1957 he moved to Dorchester where he joined the Dorset Natural History and Archaeological Society and contributed a number of articles to their *Proceedings*. He wrote several Dorset Monographs and also contributed articles to *Somerset & Dorset Notes & Queries*, the *Archaeological Newsletter*, and the *Proceedings* of the Prehistoric Society. He was a founder member of Dorset Record Society and remained active in local research until his death in 1976.[1] His interest in the Rackett Papers may have begun with a curiosity to learn about his birthplace, as the Papers include letters from Anna Maria Blunt, who was living at Enham House in the 1820s.

Thomas Rackett was Rector of Spetisbury with Charlton Marshall from 1780 until his death in November 1840.[2] The survival of his voluminous correspondence,

1 An obituary of H.S.L. Dewar can be found in *Proceedings of Dorset Natural History and Archaeological Society*, Vol. 97, P.6

2 His appointment probably was due to his father's friendship with Francis Fane, patron of the living at the time. *The Book of Spetisbury*, Ann Taylor, Halsgrove, 2006.

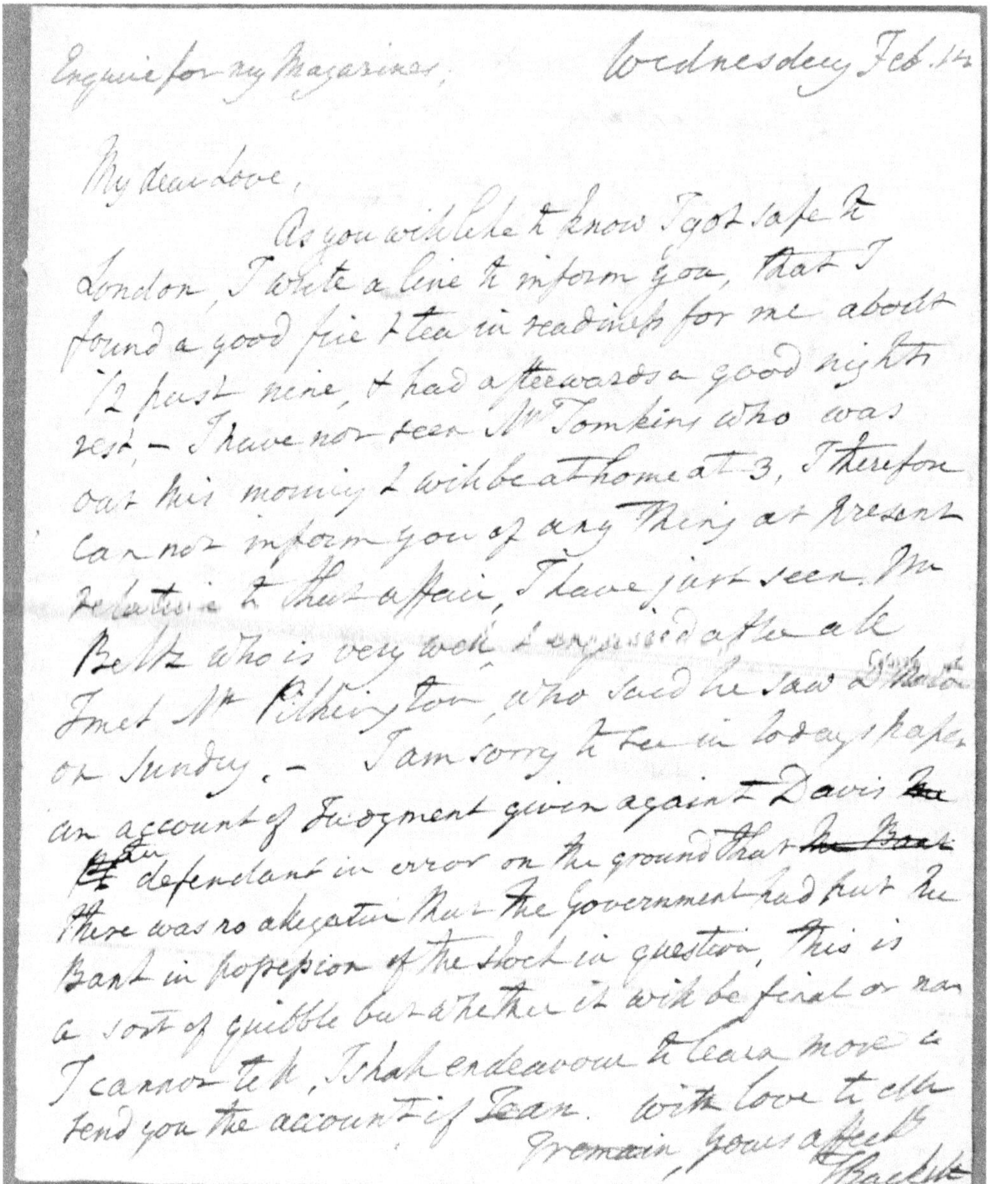

2 Letter from Thomas Rackett to his wife, 1826 [D-RAC/D/81]

collected over sixty years, is almost certainly due to his daughter, Dorothea. She accompanied her father on barrow-digging expeditions, and had various scientific interests of her own, particularly in the use of chemicals for dying fabrics. After her marriage to Samuel Solly she moved to the Midlands and was active in the foundation of the Lincoln Mechanics Institute. Her letter to her parents in October 1832, describing a public lecture by Dr Warwick (which she herself had helped to arrange), demonstrates her understanding of chemistry, physics and the new science of electricity.[3]

It is clear from her letters that Dorothea was close to her own daughter, Thomasine, and brought her up in this intellectual environment. In later life Dorothea and Samuel moved to Parkstone, where they spent their remaining years.[4] Samuel Solly died in 1847 but Dorothea lived on there with her daughter until her death in 1878. Thomasine married in 1859, but was widowed a few years later and had no children and on her death in 1882, her estate passed to her executors, one of whom was Edward Harrison Solly. In 1957 Lt. Col. R.J.N. Solly deposited the Rackett Papers in Dorset Record Office.

The text of this volume has been re-typed by Ann Smith (retaining the original spelling, capitalisation and punctuation) who also expanded the footnotes with considerable assistance from Graham Hoddinott. Despite thorough proof-reading by Graham, some errors almost certainly remain, for which she accepts sole responsibility. This volume was in preparation during the several lockdowns and restrictions during the COVID 19 pandemic, during which Dorset History Centre was either closed or had limited access. It has been possible to check some of the text against the original documents, but there may remain some discrepancies. Dewar's original footnotes have been marked (HSLD) to enable the reader to see where new material has been added. Graham undertook research into H.S.L. Dewar and the Solly family and discovered how the Papers came to be in Dorset Record Office. Mark Forrest undertook picture research and advised on overall editing. Credit for the attractive look and feel of the book goes to John Chandler, who typeset and indexed the text and has put together the finished volume.

Ann Smith

3 It is interesting to note from the Rackett Papers how women were treated as intellectual equals; in his letter to Mrs Rackett in February 1834, Charles Hatchett explores in some detail the Hebrew, Greek, Latin and German origins of the term 'Breeches' in the Bible, obviously continuing an earlier conversation with her.
4 1841 Census HO107/287/6, Fol. 26, P. 16

3, 4, Two views of Spetisbury Rectory [RCHM]

D-RAC/A/18. Letter from John Cutler to his Sister Abigail Caillouel.

(No address, but almost certainly from Boston, Mass.)
Novr. ye 4: 1754.
Dr. Sister,
I recd. yours without Date thoug gues at it by Being Inclosd; in my News Lettr. ? I rejoyce to hear you are well & that my Neice is so well provided for & has got so good & agreeable a Companion. Pray God to Bles them & Continue them Long and Happy together: I am Glad you have done with that worthless fellow. You writ to me for an attested Certyficate of his marriage to his first wife here which I have had no Time to Inquire after since I Recd. yours: By reason of my Ilnes & am now But Ill abell to set to write but was Loath to Mis this opportunity: The man yt. Married him I Believe is now in England has a living at Lee, his name is Roger Price, if his mariage Is upon Record I will Inquire & if can will Git It attested & send It to you – I writ you some time since about a Book wrote by Isbrand Idis[1]: he was Ambasidor from Mosco to China Sent by Peter Ye Great Czr. of Moscvy. It is possible you may Lite of it among Your second Hand Books I suppose it is out of print for I never saw but one of them & that was Stole from me Reading Mr Hannoways Travels to Persia[2] I had a mind to see something In that Book if you git Mr Lane will pay for it I writ for a Velvet Cap at same time if you git he will pay for them.

I have nothing to ad But my kind Love & Good wishes for yr Health and Remain
Yr. Loving Brother
Jno Cutler.

D-RAC/A/18. Letter from John Cutler to Mrs Abigail Caillouel.

Boston June ye 18th 1755
I recd. yr. kind letter By Capt. Jno. Phillips & Rejoyced to hear yours and yr. families welfare & to thank Mr. Racket for ye. Book and cap which came safe – I have writ before to thank him But perceive yr. Lettr. never came to hand: I take this Being the first opportunity since I recvd. yours to let you that we are still in ye. Land of the Living though both of us invalides. Your sister not able to walk alone Nor myself without Crutch But I thank Mr Racket for his kind invitation as much as .... wd ....

1 Eberhard Isbrand Ides, Danish traveller, 1660-1700. (HSLD) He wrote an account of the Gobi Desert which was published in French translation in 1718.
2 Jonas Hanway (1712-1786), *Account of British Trade in the Caspian Sea with a Journal of Travels*, 1753.

able to come & se you which would be a pleasure not to be exprest: I shall write you in a few days by a Gentlewoman who is coming by way of Bristol for Holland: And has promised to come and see you: her name is Sarah Todd with whom Molly Haywood lived till she died and is a worthy woman and nottable trader she will be able to inform you more than I can write as to .... Here is a Large armament and expedition Going forward as yet not come to action, one Regiment marchd last week: & one went about a fortnight ago to ye. Estward to endeavour to .... Nova Scotia & Coll. Peperall's Regitt & Col. Sherly's & the Virginia forses all to ye. Westward and Hope providence will give them success to curb the insolence of ye. worst of Enymies ye. French & Indians of which I think ye. French ye. worst.

I am sorry to hear any belonging to our family should behave in so scoundrell a manner As to deserve ye. place that vile wretch is in and wish he may not deserve a wors: When I first heard of his being confin'd which Capt. Phillips writ of. Did not know but it was on your acct., which he highly deserv'd I am sorry his sister has not answer'd your Letter I take her to be quite different temper and Behaves very well she is married again to one Johnno a Frenchman and has two children by him & 3 By Mr Johnson, though has been much abused by her Brother by his writing but wht. he says or writes Goes for Littel ....

We have had an open winter here but Long and at Present a very Promising season for plenty of fruit of which we had none last year But apples; neither Pear Plum or Cherry: If anything happens worth remark Between this & my next shall let you know. In the Mean Time Et.
Jno. Cutler

D-RAC/A/18. Letter from John Cutler, her brother, to Mrs Abigail Caillouel

Boston. July 3rd 1755
This comes by Captt. Cahale by whome I shall send a small Box to be left with Mr Lane where you may call for it: In which is a Ring for Mr. Racket which I desire he will Accept of us as a small token of my Respect & the 30 Guinees Desire you will accept of, And when you write Desire you will take no farther notis only the Rectt of mine by Capt Cahale, and if it is not to much Troubell to get me a Dozen of India Mangoes & send them to Mr Lanes who will pay ye Oyleman Let them be put in a stone Pot and Close Stopt, & Directed for me, Mrs Tod By whom I design'd these Sailed sooner than she Expected so Mist ye portunity: But hope this will Reach you near as soon; we are like to have ye seat of ye War with us this Summer Here is a Squadron of French men of War of 13 some say 15 Sail & Admiral BosCowen with 12 Sail he has taken 2 French Men of War One of 64 & one of 74 Guns with a great Number of Troops on Board & 15000 in Cash so if we have a War will be a good Capture We lost but 2 men & about 7 or 8 wounded in taking ye forts which is a remarkable instance of ye Good Providence of God Beyond what could be expected: I hope shall have an opportunity to give you further good News in a short time: Yr Sister remains much in cold & very weak as well as myself, we cannot expect to

continue Long from age less well as Infirmity. The sixth day of Augtt I enter my 80th Year and Mrs Cutler Not a great deal short of it So Death can be no Surprise If prepared for it I hope this will find you and my Dear Now and all friends in Good Health. And Am my Dr. Sister with all sincerity.
Yr Loving Brother and Assured friend,
Jno. Cutler

D-RAC/A/18. John Cutler to Abigail Caillouel.

Boston, January ye 5 1756.
Dear Sister
I take this opportunity to let you know that your Sister & myself here in ye land of ye living Though a few weeks past we did not expect it for in ye 17 of November Last we had a most Terribell shake of an Earth Quake which shook of part of above a Thousand Chimny's Besides other damage to Severall Houses & Goods and had ye violence continued half a Minute Longer I've Thought few houses would have been left standing About 4 hours after another But not severe 5 Dayes after I had another very sensibell one But Short ye first Lasted between 2 & 3 Minutes. But through ye Goodness of Almighty God ye Preserver of all Things not a life lost of man or beast yt we hear of: Which has showed us ye Goodness of his Power: We hear in great fear what farther Melacholly Accompts we shall have from Europe, Hope it has not reached your Island. No otherwise than a warning to all People to Reform and Amend their Lives: which I pray God in his goodness, to give them Grace so to Doe: we are in .... a Melacholly condition in Respect to our Temporal Affairs: Being disappointed in our Expeditions against the French & Indians through some bad Management; where .... hope will be known in Time and Remedied .... with a suitable reward; the French & Indians are daily murthering ye poor People in ye Southern Frontiers In a most Barbarous Manner without Distinction of Age or Sex; But hope Providence will Direct some Method to Prevent them going on, or they will Brake up ye New Settlements; So much for news: Since I began this Hour Capt. Brand is arrived & if I have no Lettr. By him I shall conclude .... [words missing here Ed.] .... ordinary has happened .... is returned By whom I design'd my Lettrs. & she promised to come & see you but for want of knowing where you Lived Though she Lodged in yr. Neighbourhood did not; for which I am very Sorry For I am sure you would have been pleased with her .... I have nothing to send at Present But my Love and Good Wishes for my Nephew and Niece, And king Love for
My Dear Sister from your Loving
Brother Jno. Cutler

D-RAC/J/145. Letter from T. Cavallo[3] to Rev. T. Rackett

September the 8th 1786.
Dear Sir,
It is an age since I received a letter of yours. Are you perhaps offended at my not coming to Spetesbury? – Forgive me this time, and next Summer if you please, I shall come to stay at direction.

The principal object of this letter is to recommend to your hospitality and civility a Knight errant, the Chas. ~~Hache~~, of the order of the short stick and high collar. It being the very spirit of Knight errantry to be rather eccentric, and singular, I think it is my duty to prevent your surprise by giving you some account of this otherwise worthy person.

It seems that the various scenes in which he has been engaged during his expeditions against the bearded savages of Wales, and in innumerable other situations, have somewhat disturbed his imagination, so that whenever he forgets to be in company, he exclaims with various strange phrases; and though he neither wears a wig nor feels any pain, often says "ho my wig! Oh my colic!" Then looking steady on nothing at all, and with his eyes fixed like a conjurer, says, "what a fine hair!" _ Thus my friend he feeds his imagination on the shadows of some real objects, which it is neither your nor my business to enquire after; besides which he is admirable in every respect. In music he is a Clementi[4], (who by the bye is no longer a single man), in Chymestry he is a Bergman[5] in politeness a frenchman, and in friendship *sans pareil.* Do give me an account of his proceedings as soon as you can. How is the worthy engraver of the third order and what is she about at Present? I hardly dare to say that [I] never tried the coloured way of engraving without copper plate, which she was so good as to describe to me; but however I shall soon make a trial of it, and of something else analogous to it which *nunc mente revolvitur.*

In London there is stagnation of news, so that I have nothing to say about this subject, unless you think it worth mentioning that the King of Russia is dead and the Archduke of Milan is arrived in England, and this day dines with the King at Kew.

3 Tiberius Cavallo (1749-1809), Natural Philosopher, left Italy at an early age and settled for life in this country. He was a close friend of Thomas Rackett for over thirty years and spent prolonged periods at the Rectory in Spetisbury where a room was fitted up as a laboratory for his electrical experiments. He was friends with, the musician Clementi, the artist Paul Sandby, the astronomer William Herschell, Peter Beckford of Iwerne Stepleton and Henry Bankes of Kingston Lacy. In 1775 he published a notice of 'Extraordinary Electricity of the atmosphere observed at Islington'. He was admitted Fellow of the Royal Society in 1779. In 1786 he published his complete treatise on Electricity. After his death in 1809, Rackett was his executor.

4 Muzio Filippo Vincenzo Francesco Saverio Clementi (1752–1832). He was sponsored by Sir Peter Beckford of Iwerne Stepleton, not far from Spetisbury. He resided with Beckford from 1766-1774 and gave performances locally on the harpsichord. He moved to London in 1774 and then pursued a career abroad where he was an influence on and rival to Mozart. He returned to England in later life and died at Evesham, Worcestershire. He was a keen huntsman and kept his own pack of hounds.

5 Almost certainly T.O. Begmann, Swedish Chemist and Naturalist, 1735-1784. (HSLD)

Yours sincerely
T. Cavallo.

D-RAC/J/145. Letter from T. Cavallo Natural Philospher to Rev. Thomas Rackett

Windsor, August 13th 1786.
Dear Sir
After many considerations, disquisitions, and examinations it has been at last determined by my reasoning faculties in spite of my inclination, to march towards London in about three or four days time, and to wait for the pleasure of seeing you and Mrs. R. till you return in King Street; hoping in the meantime we may carry on a frequent literary correspondence, in order to acquaint each other with every occupation and other occurrence.

Your frequent allusions to the attraction of a lovely nature between me and some supposed Dulcinea, are like needles of reproach to my heart. It is the same thing as you were to praise a lame man for his dancing; since I very well perceive in myself a deficiency of most qualities, which may attract a female heart. I have neither flattery, nor beauty nor riches, nor &c &c.

I am very much obliged to Mrs R. for her instructions in the vegetable engraving way; but I think it requires too much trouble, and therefore I shall not attempt it at present.

As you are going to put up a sundial I must by way of practical instruction, recommend you not to place it in the shade; other instructions are needless.
Miss Herchell[6] on the first of August discovered a comet between the foot of the bear and coma berenius. I have seen it twice, or rather two nights following. It is not visible to the naked eye, but it may be easily distinguished through a telescope that magnifies at least 20 times. It has a tail, and between 9 and 10 o'clock in the evening it appears towards the N.W. and not more than 20 or 30 degrees above the horizon. It is very remarkable that this comet was not discovered on the day preceeding the attempt on the King's life[7], and that the former was discovered by a woman, as well as the latter was perpetrated by a woman. I wish that you or Mrs Jordan would endeavour to find out and ascertain the strange connection between heavenly appearances and mortal affairs, for perhaps by following the analogy we might perhaps attain to the art of foretelling human events.

I have collected three very remarkable shells for Mrs Mora's collection; namely a nut-shell, a mortar-shell and an egg-shell which I hope will be found very deserving of a place in her cabinet of curiosities.

Lately, viz: within these three months a new plant has been brought from China

6 Miss Caroline Lucretia Herschel (1750-1848), astronomer, 8th child of Isaac Herschel and Anna Ilse Moritzen. The comet, mentioned by Cavallo which she discovered on 1st August 1786, was looked at with curiosity by Miss Burney as 'the very first lady's comet'. (D.N.B.) (HSLD)

7 On 2 August 1876 Margaret Nicholson attempted to stab George III with an ivory-handled dessert-knife. She appears to have been mentally unstable.

to England. It is called the lemon grass, because it smells strongly of lemon when rubbed between the fingers, as you may perceive from the enclosed specimen, which I hope will preserve the smelling property when dry. The great use which they make of it is to make agreeable infusions of it in water for convalescence to drink. Dr. Lind[8] has got one plant of it, and one day we put some tea in the teapot, and I assure you it gave the tea a very agreeable.

Scarceness of news, and a necessity of going upon terrass with some friends who are now hurrying me, oblige me to put an end to the letter, and therefore I conclude with subscribing myself.
Engraver the 2d and 3d
The humble servant and friend
T. Cavallo.
P.S. Please to direct your next for me in London.

D-RAC/E/102. Letter from Charles Hatchett[9] to Rev. Th. Rackett.

St. Petersbourg Octr. 30th 1790
Dear Rackett
I make no doubt that you have received the letter which I wrote to you from Elbing, it was my intention to have written again before now, but the multiplicity of my other letters and the inconvenience of the road have prevented me. On the 17th of Sept (?) we left Elbing and after travelling through the worst road imaginable by way of Brounsberg, Hopenbrock, and Brandenbourg in Royal Prussia, we reached Konigsberg the Capital on 18 by dinner time. There is nothing worthy of the notice of a traveller at Konigsberg, it is very extensive, unelegant and dirty, and the trade is much the same as at Dantzig and Elbing. It was founded in 1254 by Primislaus III, King of Bohemia who had conquered a considerable part of Royal Prussia from its Pagan inhabitants.

We set out from Konigsberg on the 19 for Memel, after having gone about 20 English miles from Konigsberg the road is continued on a sand bank 86 miles in length and breadth from 1 to 3 miles, the Baltic surrounds it on every side excepting near Konigsberg and it is separated from Memel by a haven in some places a mile and in others half a mile broad. It is perfectly barren unless at two post houses situated on the further side of the bank, here indeed are a few fir trees which with difficulty seem to grow, all the rest is barren and consists of sand shells and stones. The road is

8 Probably Dr. James Lind M.D. (1736-1812), as he visited China when he was a surgeon in an East Indiaman in 1766. He had a 'love of Eastern wonders .... tricks, conundrums and queer things', according to Mme. D'Arblay (Miss Burney). (HSLD)

9 Charles Hatchett (1765-1847) mineralogist and analytical chemist, member of the Royal Society and Linnaean Society, who discovered the element niobium. Two mineral substances, one discovered in the USA, the other in Australia, were named after him. On his father's death he gave up chemistry and succeeded him as coachbuilder to the king. He was at school with Thomas Rackett and was a lifelong friend. He lived at Mount Clare House, Roehampton and later at Belle Vue House, Cheyne Walk, Chelsea.

close to the waters edge and the wheels of my carriage were more than once deeply washed by The waves of the Baltic. At this place the Duchess of Kingston was once overset and was in some danger of being drowned. We did not arrive at the end of the Bank till 3 o'clock on the Sept. 21st and after having with difficulty gotten into the boat we were ferried over by 6 women who very much resembled (in their loquacity and impudence) our amiable Ladies at Billingsgate. I had great civilities shown me by the British Consul at Memel from whence we departed on the 22nd Septr. and after crossing a small part of Lithuania we entered Courland and arrived at Mittau[10] the Capital on the 25, - There is not anything attractive of curiosity in Mittau unless it is the Ducal Palace which is an enormous pile of building much too extensive and magnificent for such a town as Mittau and so petty a Duchy as Courland.

The present Duke is son of the Count Biren created Duke of Courland by the Empress Anne, and the present Duke accompanied his father into Siberia where he was arrested and banished by Anne the Regent. The deposed Duke of Courland (Prince Charles of Saxony) is at the Court of Dresden, and the Present Duke is far from being on good terms with his present subjects and Nobles.

We set out from Mittau on the 25th and having passed through Courland and enter'd Livonia we reached Riga on the 26th. Riga altho' the Capital of what is called the granary of Europe, is situated in the midst of barren sand, but its situation being commodious for trade has occasioned the foundation of the City which is attributed to some Merchants of Bremen who founded Riga on the banks of the Dvina in the 12 or 13 century. The bridge across the Dvina is in length about 900 paces: it is built on pontoons and is constructed so as to rise and fall with the tide. The Gates of the City still retain the arms and the crown of Sweden with the Cypher of Charles the eleventh. The principal Merchant in Riga (Mr Pierson) behaved to me with the greatest hospitality and .... I departed perfectly satisfied with my reception. [About two lines at the bottom of the page are largely illegible owing to the leaf being damaged. Ed]

D-RAC/E/102. Letter from Charles Hatchett (Chemist and Mineralologist) to Rev. Thomas Rackett.

24 Feb. Moscow. March 7th 1791[11].
Dear Rackett

10 Mitau, or Jelgava. (HSLD)

11 Hatchett dates his letter according both to the Julian and Gregorian calendars. The Julian calendar had been introduced by Julius Caesar, but by the later middle ages it was realized that the calendar year was increasingly divergent from the solar year, due to a slight miscalculation. This was remedied by a Papal Bull of Pope Gregory in 1582, which cut out 10 days to bring the calendar in line, and avoided future difficulties by adjusting the number of leap years in each century. Britain, which had recently broken from the church in Rome, declined to follow, and it was not until 1752 that the Gregorian calendar was adopted, by which time it was necessary to omit eleven days. The Orthodox Church continued to use the old calendar, and it was not until the twentieth century that Russia, the Balkan States and Greece adopted the reformed calendar, by which time it was necessary to take out nearly two weeks.

I have waited in the hopes of hearing from you till my patience has been completely exhausted. Your vocations at Spetisbury can never take up so much of your time as to prevent you from writing now and then to your friends, particularly one who is removed to so great a distance as I am. I however now begin to be on the move and hope in the course of the spring or summer to arrive in England. I quitted St. Petersbourg last week and found the roads to this city very indifferent on account of the small quantity of snow which renders the roads less proper for sledges. Petersbourg is yet very unfinished and exhibits a mixture of Palaces and cottages which is not to be equalled anywhere except in this place where it is far exceeded in respect to the public establishments and seminaries (all of which have been open to my inspection without reserve). I shall at a future time give you full information by means of accounts which I have written and which are amongst my papers: they would be too extensive to be inserted in letters even if treated of in a concise manner. I have found Professor Pallas[12] a most friendly and communicative man, free from all pedantry and always ready to render service; his travels through this immense Empire are too well known to need any comment. Through him I have procured a fine collection of Siberian ores particularly those of gold and silver, as well as of his Flora Rossica, the Vocabulary etc. Since I have been here I have met with a large number of MSS. brought from Thibet, Tangut, Etc. which treat of the Mythology of the Mongols, their elements of Education, their science, their various dialects, and their arts, if I should perchance meet with any one skilled in Oriental languages in England who will undertake to translate them there is no doubt that much light would be thrown on their religious opinions Etc. Through the kindness of Dr. Pallas I have also formed a complete collection of the Calmuck and Mongol Idols in Bronze and clay with others painted on silk, these which were collected by him during his travels & are much to be valued as they are not to be met with in any collection either public or private except in that of the Acad. des Sciences at Petersbourg of which these are duplicates. No regular accounts have been yet received of Billings[13] who is gone on a voyage of discovery from the coast of Kamtchatka, only it is certain that one of his two vessels was lost in going out of the port of Ochotsk [Okhotsk]. When I write next I shall be able to give you some account of Moscow as I have letters of the Orlovs [Orloffs] and all the principal families. Moscow is more an Asiatic that a European city in appearance, but several matters have been much misrepresented which I will mention another time. I hope Mr., Mrs. and Mrs T.R. with the dear little Boy[14] and girl are well, pray remember me to them and also Mr Ickytts family, Mr Harris, my friend Yetman the Bold, and all

12 Prof. P.F. Pallas, German Naturalist and traveller, 1741-1811. (HSLD)

13 Probably Joseph Billings, explorer, (who sailed under Capt. Cook on his last voyage) and Lieutenant of the Russian Navy. (HSLD)

14 Dorothea, daughter of Thomas Rackett was baptized at St Paul's Covent Garden in 1787. Thomas, son of Rev. Thomas Rackett was baptized at Spetisbury on 2 December 1789. William Tattersall, son of Rev. Thomas Rackett was baptized at Spetisbury on 3 August 1791. No burials have been found, but as neither of the sons is mentioned again, it may be assumed that they did not survive infancy.

friends. Mrs. H. joins in best respects .... behaved.... like a heroine.

D-RAC/E/102. Letter from Charles Hatchett to Rev. Th. Rackett.

Cracow July 24th 1791
Dear Rackett
It was my intention to have written to you long ago either from Kiow or Warsaw, but various matters have prevented me .... our journey from Moscow to Tula was easily performed, and I had the satisfaction of seeing the Imperial Fabrick at Tula for arms and steel wares, they employ about 2000 men, although some have exaggerated so far as to say 6000. I had letters to the Governor who was very polite. From Tula to Kiow [Kiev] the road was very bad by reason of the rains and the richness of the soil, particularly in Ukraine. The situation of Kiow is very romantic, being on the banks of the Dneiper and built (in respect of the old town) on high cliffs. I need scarcely mention to you that it is the most antient city in Russia and was the Capital till Daniel son of Alexander Nevski in 1304 transferred the seat of Government to Moscow. The City is divided into 3 parts Viz., 1st, the Old Town, 2nd, the New Town and 3rdly the Podol, or Low Town. Most of the buildings are of wood except the Churches and Monasteries. The most remarkable is the Cathedral of St. Sophia built in 1037 by Iaroslaf Vladimirovitch, he employed Greek Architects etc. from Constantinople, and the inside of the dome is ornamented with mosaic figures not badly executed when the date is consider'd and the state of the arts at that time. I was introduced to the Arch Bishop a venerable old man and very amiable in his manners as well as replete with information. I went afterwards to the Monastery of Petcherski founded in the 10th century by St. Antonius & St. Theodosius. This Monastery is chiefly remarkable for the Catacombs which bear the names of the two above mentioned Saints. They are excavated in the mountain and are of considerable extent, there are in them a great number of niches in each of which is a dried Saint dressed in rich robes and one of the hands uncover'd to be kissed by the pilgrims and other devout people: amongst others is the famous Nestor who may justly be called the parent of Russian History. I received great civilities as well as Mrs. H. from young Prince and princess Daschkow. I had also letters for the General Governor, who was at first very civil, but a little before my departure took it into his head that I was a spy and in consequence gave me some trouble. We passed a couple of days at Biala Czerkow with the Countess Bramitski the wife of the Grand General of Poland: from this place we went to the City of Lublin which contains nothing remarkable unless it is the monument of the Union of Poland and Lithuania which was finally established in 1569 under Sigismund Augustus in a general Diet held at Lublin. During our stay at Warsaw I visited everything worthy of notice, such as the Public Library founded by the Zaluski's, but which for want of revenue has remained (word illegible here. Ed.) near 20 years. The collection of medals is very good particularly those of Greece and Rome which are complete. Amongst the latter are several Otho's in high preservation, and the medals of Vespasian, Titus and Domitian struck in the taking of Jerusalem and bearing the

inscription *Iudea Capta.* All the three are very scarce, but those of Titus and Domitian so in particular. In looking over the medals and antiquities I had the advantage of having with me the Abbe Albertrandi[15] the King's Librarian and Keeper of the medals, a man of great learning in general but particularly in Antiquities. Warsaw as a city is *triste* but the society renders it pleasant, there is no place where Gallantry is more general (not excepting Venice) and if an Island, Warsaw might be named the modern Paphos. The Revolution has been well received by all ranks, and Poland hitherto the prey to Anarchy, Confusion and civil discord may now hope for better days. The Poles certainly cannot have a better monarch than the present as his goodness of heart can only be equalled by his talents which was clearly demonstrated on the 3rd of May. As I am not curious in respect of Courts I intended to have passed quietly through Warsaw, but his Majesty did me the honour to send for me, and after I had been presented told me that he loved and respected the English, and that he should have been concerned to have heard that an Englishman had passed Warsaw without his having seen him: I afterwards dined with him at his Palace of Lazienki[16] where there was in the evening a Ballet, and took my leave some days afterwards with great regret. The road from Warsaw to Cracow was nothing interesting, but near Cracow the Country is more varied than that about Warsaw. Cracow preserves the appearance of a city formerly handsome but is now deserted; it still retains the marks of the late intestine troubles, many of the houses etc., bearing the marks of cannonading. The old Palace has been totally ruined on the inside, but has lately been repaired. The Cathedral contains the tombs of the Kings of Poland beginning with Casimir the Great. The Body of St. Stanislaus Arch Bishop of Cracow who was murdered at the foot of the Altar by Boleslaus the Hardy reposes in a silver shrine in the middle of the Church. I said Warsaw was *triste* but Cracow may be called the very *sejour* of everything dismal. I have visited the Salt mines of Wiclieza and was let down at the end of a rope (much as you have seen the sign of the Golden Fleece) about 240 Paris feet, but for an account of this I refer you to a letter which I shall write on the subject to our friend Cavallo. Make our best respects to all the family and remember me to his Boldship, the Ickyll family, Mrs Harris, Etc. I am Dear Rackett with great regard,

Your affectionate friend and Servant

Ch. Hatchett.

Do write as soon as you receive this and direct your letter to me at Messrs. J.G. Schuller & Co., Vienna, and say where Miss Furst lives and her present name, I have mislaid your letter. I find I cannot make this serve as a cover and therefore shall continue my letter. Do not forget when you write to say how you are, as well as the rest of the family: I suppose by this time you have a small trio. In case Mrs. R. should see my mother, beg of her to keep up her spirits. We are now jogging homeward but it would be idle to travel so far and not profit by it in respect to information. I hope it will not be long before we meet again in England.

D-RAC/E/102. Letter from Chas. Hatchett to Rev. Th. Rackett.

15 Jan Chrzcicet Albertrandy: Polish numismatist, 1731-1808. (HSLD)

16 Leszczyncki. (HSLD)

Edinburgh July 2nd – 1796 –
Dear Rackett,
The perpetual whirl I have been in ever since we parted, and the desire to collect some interesting matter of information for you, may perhaps afford an excuse (altho' a bad one) for not writing to you before, but indeed had I written to you concerning the first part of my Tour, I would have added little to that with which you were already acquainted.

In respect to Cornwall I have therefore little to say in the Philosophical way, as to that which was comical, I must tell you that Savaresi being urged by curiosity to inspect a China Beaker placed on a high Chimney Piece at the Redruth Hotel, emptied a quantity of Liquid into his mouth and over his clothes, the quality of which was speedily announced by his sputtering and exclaiming with a rueful visage "C'est de l'Urine" ....

From Cornwall we passed through the North of Devon which from Maton I understood you also visited. We then went to Taunton, Bridgewater, Cheddar Cliffs, Wells and at length rested for a few days at Bath. Here again I had the pleasure to meet Maton but by some mistake was prevented from taking leave of him. During our stay at Bath, I particularly examined the Bath stone. It is essentially different from that of Purbeck, and of Portland, or the first is a species of Lumachella[17] and the second is a Calcareous Grit. The Bath stone on the contrary is a true oolithes, or an aggregation of small calcareous globules like the Pisoliths[18] of Carlsbad and the Hammites[19] or Ketton stone of Rutlandshire, only that the Globules composing the Bath stone are even smaller than those of the Ketton stone.

From Bath we went to Bristol, where with that true narrow spirit which characterises the Bristol People, we were not suffered to see any of their works, and lost on that account two full days. I vented my spleen by writing a Sonnet on the walls of my apartment which I will send you in a future letter.

The Limestone which composes the chief part of St. Vincents Rocks[20], is for the greater part very Bitumenous and like that which I noticed at Kimmeridge is occasionally intersected by veins of grey Silex which often passes into Petro Silex[21].

From Bristol we proceeded to Glocester, Tewkesbury, Worcester and Birmingham; I did not meet with any matter worthy of observation (excepting the Porcelain works at Worcester) till we arrived at Birmingham. The works at this place interested me much, altho' (like everything else) they are much injured and damped by the progress by the war. From Birmingham we went by Wednesbury (where are

17 Lumachella, or Shelly limestone. (HSLD)

18 Pisoliths, or Pisolites. (HSLD)

19 Hammites, or Ammonites. (HSLD)

20 Part of the Avon Gorge, the Rocks were named after a hermitage, cave and chapel of St Vincent. In this area quartz crystals known as Bristol Diamonds are found and there are warm springs which were developed in the 18th century into a Spa and pump room. This area of Bristol is still known as Hotwells.

21 Literally translated as 'rock flint', the term relates to any hard or igneous rock.

several Coal Pits and Forges) to Wolverham'ton and from there to Coalbrook Dale.

I do not recollect that I ever was so much struck with any place in my life as with this last. In saying this, I do not merely mean the aspect of the Country (which however is highly Romantic and Picturesque) but I combine at the same time the Natural History of it, and the wonderfully extensive works there stablished for smelting and forging of iron. The Natural Phenomena are very remarkable; for instance, Iron Ore, Coal, and Limestone are found almost together in the greatest abundance and of the best quality; so that this Place seems purposely to have been made for Iron Works. I even found coal on the Iron Ore which is certainly very singular, and the Iron Ore is no less remarkable, in itself as the greater part is more or less filled with remains and impressions of vegetables as well as Marine Animals. At about one mile from the Dale is a spring which continually affords a considerable quantity of pure petroleum.

I do not say anything of the Iron Bridge because you have undoubtedly seen Drawings or Plates of it, otherwise I certainly should not pass over a work so beautiful in its appearance and so extraordinary in its construction.

The Iron Works are upon a most extensive scale, particularly those belonging to the Reynolds and to the family of Darby (all Quakers), but beside these the number of others is so great that at night a man might fancy himself on the Borders of the Infernal Regions. From Coalbrook Dale we went to Newcastle under Line and from there visited Etruria the celebrated Pottery of Mr Wedgwood. We then proceeded to Derby where we saw the Slitting[22] Mills and other apparatus of the Marble Works[23].

At Warkworth we were not permitted to see the Cotton Mills as Mr Arkwright[24] was not at home, and we therefore immediately proceeded to Matlock. This is a beautiful Romantic little spot and would afford food for your Pencil. The Limestone of which the Mountain is chiefly composed, is Bitumenous with veins and stratifications of Silex. The Toad stone[25] is also found here and is the substance through which the waters of the Baths flow. These Waters have no perceptible Taste and are of 68° Temperature. I shall farther observe that Matlock is very quiet and a very lounging place.

At Ashover we were received with great Politeness by the Agent of Sir Josh Banks, and with him we visited the Lead Mines. Ones of these called West Edge is remarkable for the quantity of Slicken Sides[26] which it affords. In another Mine called Gregory Hillock celebrated for the great profit it has yielded, is a Singular Phenomenon. A considerable quantity of Water flows from the Vein which has even been safely Drunk by the Miners, but if perchance a drop happens to touch their eyes, a Violent inflammation ensues and for some days they become Blind. Some of the Water has been just sent to Sir J. Banks to be analysed.

22 Marble does not 'split' readily, and is often described as being 'slit' into slabs.

23 Richard Brown established marble works in Derby in about 1735 and several generations of the family ran the works. They pioneered methods of sawing the stone which were much admired by visitors.

24 Richard Arkwright, inventor of spinning Jenny, 1755-1843. (HSLD)

25 Toad stone, a provincial name for a volcanic rock with almond –shaped nodules. (HSLD)

26 Slicken Slides: polished sides of a fault plane. (HSLD)

In going from Ashover to Bakewell we visited Chatsworth which fell very short of my expectations. At Bakewell Mr White Watson took considerable pains to shew us everything Worthy of Notice, which by the bye was not much. At Buxton our next stage, we visited Pooles Hole a cavern of the same Nature, but in some respects inferior in my opinion to Kents Hole[27]. In our way to Buxton we visited the celebrated Ecton Mine[28] and entered it by a Level at the foot of the Mountain. This Mine affords Lead, Copper, and Blende, the latter they did not know till I pointed it out. The Temperature of the Buxton Waters is more considerable than that of Matlock as it is 82°.

Our next stage was Castleton, but as I have not room here to do it justice, and you must be fatigued with so long a journey, I shall now take off the Horses that you may repose. In a future letter we shall set it out again. I have been here five days and have paid my visits and deliver'd my Credentials to Dr. Black and other Professors. As to the City and other Matters I shall not here anticipate them but shall give you a full and true account in the regular progress of our Journey. Savaresi is gone back, being recalled by reason of the adverse State of affairs in Italy.

In about a week I shall set out for the Highlands. Pray make my best respects to both of the Ladies, to your Father, and also to Dr. and Mrs. Pultenay.

There will be £24.3.2. due to you the 10th of this Month on the £1610.14. 8/3 Pr. Ct. Consols[29], which as I shall not be in the way to receive, I shall desire my Father to remit to you out of my Monies, and I can receive it and consequently be reimbursed on my return. You need not object to this as it will make no difference to me till called for. Be so good as to write as soon as possible, and direct your Letter to me, to remain at the Post Office at Glasgow I shall thus receive it on my return from the Highlands.
I am, Dear Rackett,
Yours with the greatest regard,
Chas. Hatchett.

D-RAC/J/145. Letter from T. Cavallo to Rev. T. Rackett.

August the 7th 1797.
Dear Sir,
I received your favour of the 19th of July when I was just going to advertise for you in the news paper, as for people lost in a fog, in a pond, in a river in the Devil's a — or in some other devilish bad place. I was of course very much delighted to find that, *post tot tantosque labores,* the three poor mariners had at last reached the promised land, which is flowing with — (you may add what).

Your concise account of the journey and of the wonders which you saw,

27 Kent's Cavern in Torquay
28 Ecton copper mine, Staffordshire
29 Three per cent Consolidated Annuities issued by the Bank of England. First issued in 1751, the interest rate had been reduced to 3% in 1757, and the last Consols were not finally redeemed until 2015 in accordance with the *Finance Act 2015*.

deserves my best thanks as it has excited my curiosity as well as my inventive powers; in consequence of which many questions to be asked, and many plans to be communicated hereafter, are now kept in store for you. One observation however I shall take the liberty to mention, which is that Dr. Sh—d's picture with globes, rulers etc., is, in my humble opinion, improperly placed in the public library, and that its proper place would be the Devil's a— in Derbyshire.

I hope Mrs. Rackett's eye-sockets are not tired with seeing so many fine things. As for Miss Dagerwood, I know she is never tired of seeing and being seen. I shall be glad to hear all their remarks, observations, descriptions and conclusions. Your representation *ad vivium* of the prospects &c. must likewise add to the pleasure of our winter evenings lucubrations. I am glad to hear that the conjuring box arrived safe, and hope you have made good use of it; viz. for finding latitudes, measuring distances, drawing views, setting fire to haystacks, &c. &c.

I am very much flattered by Mrs. Pearson's expressing a disappointment at not seeing me with you, and I would add many fine sentiments and expressions, if I were sure of not being challenged. At all events I shall leave this business to Mrs. Rackett's discretion and friendship, requesting her to say whatever she thinks proper in my name whenever she writes to the *ci-devant* Miss J—.

I shall now turn a new leaf, and shall say something about myself, which however can all be comprised into a very few lines. It is about a month since I came to Black Heath, from whence I have the honour and pleasure of writing the present incoherent epistle. Previous to this excursion, and since you left Town, I was but once at the Opera. *Nina*[30] was the talk of the performance and Benti sung charmingly in it. My occupations at this place have been various, but not unusual, viz., writing, reading, playing cards and mechanical operations. The object of those mechanical operations was a most extraordinary Baby-house, which my young friends of black heath have been decorating with great expence and ingenuity, in order to present it to a young lady of their acquaintance. Notwithstanding the assistance of the cabinet maker, and toy shop, it has cost nearly six months work. I beg you will tell my friend Dorothea that the above mentioned Baby-house consisted of four rooms, viz. a kitchen, a parlour, a drawing room, and bed room. Every article is in itself complete and in the proportion of one inch to a foot, when compared with the building and furniture of a real large house. The productions of my hands are the following, viz. a pair of screens for the drawing room, an ink stand with wafer[31], and sand boxes, sealing wax, &c., The brass door nocker, the brass door plate with the name engraved on it, the books for the book-case, and several other articles of less note.

I came to this place on so short a notice that I had no time to take leave of your mother, nor have I heard of her since, but I shall probably go to Town in the course of the week, and shall immediately call upon her. The weather has been very showery about London, excepting indeed four or five days of very hot weather. If the same has

30 *Nina*, by Giovanni Paisiello was first performed in Italy in 1789.

31 A wafer-box was a writing accessory – it held the wafers used to seal letters. The sand-box contained blotting sand; paper ink blotters did not become popular until the latter half of the 19th century.

been the case in your part of the country you must have had very little opportunity of getting out. Sincerely wishing you as well as Mrs. R. and Miss, health and happiness. I remain
Yours sincerely
T. Cavallo.

D-RAC/C/37. Letter from George Harris to Rev. T. Rackett.

? Nouvelly, Feby. 25th, 1799
It was with the truest Pleasure that I received your kind present of Dr. Brownriggs Book on Salt[32], as it came accompanied by a few Lines from my much respected friend Mrs. Rackett.

The small Pretensions I can have to the friendship of those, who are mentioned in your Letter, that I cannot but be ashamed, I am not in a Capacity to make them any other acknowledgement, but in a very full & deep sense of it. It has always been my Pride to form Acquaintances with knowing and learned men & I do not feel myself a little elated at reading the names of Messrs. Hatchett, Pearson & Maton[33], you and them must therefore excuse me, if I lay hold of this occasion of forming one with them. Permit me therefore to lay strict Injunctions on you, to return to them my thanks for these Enquiries, and my best wishes for their Health.

Dr. Brownrigg's Book contains many useful Hints some of which I think I may find of Service. The method we have of manufacturing salt in this part of the world would astonish the Dr. a little.

We boil the whole of it, in small earthen Pots, built up into a Cone, from 1500 to 2,000 Pots over one furnace. They are emptied every Six Hours and immediately filled up again with fresh Brine, which is made by drawing water from the Earth that is scraped up near the Sides of the Rivers, up which the Tide flows. On this side of India, we make no salt by solar Evaporation, though they do on the Madras Coast, and the salt consequently is larger grained, & much preferable.

With respect to Politics we have little that can be interesting, before you receive this letter, it is more than probably that we shall be engaged in another war with Tippoo Saib[34], we have an Army of 40,000 already collected in the field, under the

32 William Brownrigg (1712-1800) F.R.S., medical doctor, chemist and scientist. He published *The Art of Making Common Salt* in 1748.

33 Dr. William George Maton, (1774-1835), physician and writer. His services in connection with compiling information for the second edition of Hutchins' *History of Dorset*, are acknowledged by Gen. John Belasis in the Preface to that work. (HSLD) He studied medicine and was physician to the Westminster Hospital. He attended the Royal Family while they were staying in Weymouth. He was noted for his knowledge of botany. Between 1794 and 1796 he went on a tour of the West Country with Thomas Rackett and Charles Hatchett, which resulted in the publication of *Observations on the Natural History, Scenery and Antiquities of the Western Counties of England.* With Rackett he wrote *An Historical Account of Testaceological Writers*, published in the *Transactions* of the Linnaean Society.

34 Tipu Sultan (1750-1799), ruler of the Kingdom of Mysore and a pioneer of rocket artillery.

Command of General Harris[35]; our Governor, Ld. Mornington[36] is at Madras. And it is reported that Tippoo is making rapid preparations, to begin hostilities.

To all your Family pray make my kind remembrances; it is with the greatest Sincerity that I can assure you, that I hear with Pleasure of the good Health of Mrs. Rackett & yourself. Health and a contented mind renders me perfectly Happy in my present situation, and Believe me I shall be proud to subscribe myself
Your most true and most Sincere friend
George Harris.

D-RAC/C/40. Letter from Allen Fielding, son of Henry Fielding, novelist, to Rev. T. Rackett.

St. Stephens Jan. 27th 1802.
Dear Sir,
I am sorry it is not in my power to gratify you with any anecdotes of my father that will be thought worthy of place in the history of Dorset. He died so soon after my Birth that I have no knowledge of him but by tradition and the latter part of his life well known to have been such as to have furnished but little that could be agreeable to remember: tho it was in that part of his life that he produced his best works.

I take it for granted, it is known thro what channel, that little estate came into his possession. Viz, it was given by Sir Henry Gould to his daughter on her marriage with my grandfather Edmund Fielding, who possessed it during his life, after which it came to my father – who having little besides, and all the General's family viz, 4 sisters and one brother to maintain & being but little blessed with prudence and Oeconomy was soon obliged to sell it.

You ask whether an authentic account of my father has been published, to which the answer is – "certainly not". All that is to be found relative to him in print, is contained in the Life written by Arthur Murphy and prefixed to an Edition of all his books, published by Millar – Murphy himself knew nothing of my father; but patched that history up, from the accounts given to him by Millar; & a variety of good jokes that were handed about concerning him, & which would perhaps have lost much of their merit if they had been confined within the bounds of truth.

Whether the character Trulliber were drawn from Mr. Oliver or not, I am not able to say. But as so many years past between my father's being subject to a tutor, and his writing *Josh. Andrews*[37], I think his disposition does not admit of so injurious a conclusion as that he had treasured up his resentment for so many years: my Mother

---

He conducted an ongoing war with the British East India Company and was killed fighting in 1799.

35 George Harris (1746-1829), 1st Baron Harris, was appointed by Lord Mornington to command the attack on Tipu Sultan.

36 Richard Colley Wellesley (1760- 1842, 2nd Earl of Mornington, elder brother of Arthur, later Duke of Wellington. He commanded British forces at the fourth Battle of Mysore, 1798-9.

37 Henry Fielding's novel *Joseph Andrews* was published in 1742.

5 Drawings of Henry Fielding's house at East Stour by Thomas Rackett.
(Hutchins, History of Dorset, *2nd edition, vol. iii, p. 211)*

says it was not so – As to Parson Adams, being taken from Mr. Young, it is certain that most of my father's friends thought so, tho' Young himself resented the imputation so highly that he threatened to knock a gentleman down for addressing him by that name. His apartments in Chelsea Coll: were given to him by Mr. Ranby Surgeon General to the Army, merely out of regard to him, as having sat for that portrait. It was not however a very close copy – as Young possessed indeed much of Adams's simplicity and oddity, but little of his virtue. I did not know of his being editor of a Lexicon tho' he had much learning, which was the cement of my father's connexion with him. The miniature Mrs. F. left with you, is very much at your service for the use you design to make of it. – as far as I have any controll over it – it is the property of Sophia. I thank you for the anecdote of Mr. Garrick's recognizing it – it stamps an additional value on it – tho' I have always known it to be a strong likeness – my Mother is in possession of a copy of it, & values it on that account. I do not know that my Uncle Sir J.F. ever was at Stour but if ever, I dare say it was not his place of residence. My Grandfather did not reside at it, after the Death of his first wife - & Sir John was a son by his third – I hardly need to say that I wish it were in my power to give you more information on this subject as the life of such a man, may be supposed to have afforded much matter worthy of remembrance – but alas it has all perished. My wife and daughter join with me in best respects to you Mrs. & Miss Rackett – I am
Yr. Obedt. humble servt.
Allen Fielding.

D-RAC/C/39. Letter from Richard Gough[38] to Rev. T. Rackett.

Enfield. Sept. 13 1803
Dear Sr.
I am very much obliged to you for yr. communications from Gillingham, Silton &c. I hope mr. Bowle's copy of the Charter will be more correct than that of Shaftesbury. I shall be glad to have the Register carefully inspected for anecdotes. The ruins of Sturminster Newton Castle will be a great acquisition. Leland describes the Church as built by an Abbot of Glastonbury & it may also be worth drawing. I never was in it or Marnhull or Gt. Fontmell. The tracts between Blandford, Stalbridge & Shaston to extremity of the county is inexplored by me. I must therefore avail myself of the assistance of my friends.

I forget whether you have drawings of the tomb on the N. side of the altar at Tarrant Hinton or the inscription over the parsonage door.

38 Richard Gough (1735-1809), prominent antiquary and collector of manuscripts. He had interests in early coinage, Anglo-Saxon literature and mediaeval architecture. He bequeathed his large collection of books and manuscripts, along with his drawings of archaeological remains and topography to the University of Oxford, including the mediaeval Gough Map, which, is named after him. He published his two-volume *Sepulchral Monuments in Great Britain from the Norman Conquest to the 17th century* between 1786 and 1799. He was a fellow of the Society of Antiquaries and Director from 1771-1791.

I was thinking of a Plate of fonts as in the History of Worcestershire and will thank you for any additional ones to those you have already copied. I was sorry to hear that such suffering had fallen on the religious of Marnhull & Lulworth; and yet the public safety must be a primary object in these times[39]. Under the present circumstances it does not seem likely, that I should be able to visit Dorchester this year: but shall to our meeting in London & remain Dear Sr.
Yrs. faithfully,
R. Gough.

6 Drawings of Monuments at Bere Regis by Thomas Rackett[40]

39 The Hussey family of Nash Court in Marnhull remained Roman Catholics after the Reformation. The church of Our Lady was built in 1832, three years after the Catholic Emancipation Act. The Catholic church of St. Mary was built for the Weld family of Lulworth House in 1786.

40 Hutchins, *History and Antiquities of the County of Dorset*, second edition (1796-1815), Vol. I, P. 88

D-RAC/C/42. Letter from William Wood[41] to Rev. T. Rackett.

Wingham March 13th 1804.
Dear Sir,
My friend Mr. H. Boys left me the day before I received your letter on his way to Tunbridge, from whence he will go in a few days to London, where I believe he intends to practice surgery. He is in possession of all the best of his father's shells, including the minute, and I am confident he will with pleasure afford you any assistance in his power.

Mr. Boys at present lodges at Mrs. Oliver's 22 Bell Yard Carey Street. I will write to him immediately that his cabinet may be at your service whenever you think fit to make use of it. I had much information to communicate respecting the natural history of known shells which certainly was new before Mr Montague published his *testacea Britannica*[42], but he has gleaned it all, I suppose through the medium of Mr. Boys to who I communicated everything.

The brown variety of *Helix virgata* which I mentioned in a former letter, is noticed. I have only found it under the cliff about Dover. The Colonel has certainly been indefatigable in his researches into the Natural History of British shells and his work will doubtless be of great service to future conchologists. One thing however I must put you upon your guard about. The *Turbo cinctus* which Mr. Montague received from Sandwich was not found upon our shore, but purchased by Mr. Boys in the neighbourhood of Moorfields. I was with him at the time and bought several specimens which I have no doubt were foreigners. It is more than probable that he forgot the circumstance and sent the shell to the Colonel as a native.

I have a shell in my cabinet which I consider as distinct from the fresh water muscles [sic] I have hitherto seen. The specimen was sent me by Mr. Shaw from the Bexley river, and is the only one I could ever procure. It agrees in some respects with the *Mytilus avonensis* of Mr. Montague, but does not appear from his description to be the same shell. The shell is of an olivaccous brown colour with strong concentric *striae* decorticated about the hinge. Length an inch and three quarters, Breadth two inches ten lines. The front margin is sub-arcuated. This species is much thicker than the *M: Anatinus,* and my specimen weighs 6 drams 64 grains whereas *M: Anatinus* which I have at this moment on the table, and which is of the same length though much broader, weighs barely two drams. I have merely traced one valve of this shell to give you an idea of the shape. In Mr. Boys collection you will see both the *Venus Pallastra* and *decussata,* and it may not be amiss to tell you, that the latter shell is to be found alive & in great Perfection among the muscles before they are cleaned which are brought in abundance to Lumber Court, Seven Dials, where Mr. Boys and myself found all our specimens. I cannot give you any information about Mr. Walker as I

41 William Wood (1745-1808) was a Unitarian minister and botanist who contributed to several encyclopaedia.

42 George Montagu (1753-1815) published *Testacea Britannica* or *The Natural History of British Shells* in 1803. He was also known for his pioneering work in classifying British birds and some species are named after him.

never heard his name mentioned except by Mr. Boys. I believe Mr. Boys has collected many varieties of *Turbo bidens* & *perversus*, but if you should not be satisfied with his collection I shall be happy to send you any I possess. Present my kind compliments to Dr, Maton and believe me
Dr. Sir, Yours very sincerely,
Wm. Wood.

It will give me much pleasure to hear from you again, and more to see both you and Dr. Maton in this part of the world, if your leisure will permit you to spend a few days with me. Shall we have a Volume, this spring?

D-RAC/E/105. T. Cavallo, Natural Philosopher to Dorothea Rackett

Newick, December 8th 1805
Many thanks to you My Dear Dorothea, for the various, important and pleasing news, with which your favour of the 21st Ulto, is replete. Your account is so very clear, proper, and methodical, as to betray the hand of a mathematician; and if ever I become an Emperor like Buonaparte, I shall certainly bestow upon you the title of historian to my imperial majesty.

I am very glad to hear that Miss Foster is to become a Saint, and congratulate you on account of the employment you are to have on that occasion: the celebration of which, I hope, will be attended with general satisfaction, and will be followed by prosperity and happiness: but take care that you do not choke yourself with bride cake, by ramming it all in your own mouth; and not saving a piece some friend of yours, now at Newick, who is not married; for though I do not know the precise vertue of that renowned cake; yet I have always heard that a piece of it, which has been passed through the wedding ring is, really and truly , possessed of the most extraordinary virtues. Having not heard anything more of the duel you mention, and not having found any account of it in the newspapers, I am induced to hope that the Irish courage was cooled in time to prevent it by the snow of Dorsetshire. We have had no snow here, and no cold weather, to which I must thankfully add, that I am perfectly free from cough or oppression of my lungs. My intention was to be in Town by the end of November; but intentions and events, though nearly related, seldom agree, witness the performance of Blue Beard at a certain place, also the survey of a field at the same place, &c &c. What has principally detained me at this place, longer than I at first intended, is the expectation of Mr. and Mrs. Hastings, who have promised to come and spend two or three days with Sir Elijah's family, and to whom Sir E.[43] wishes to introduce me; however, if they do not come in the course of the next week, I think, I shall set off for London on the beginning of next week so as to be in Town by the

43 Sir Elijah Impey, Chief Justice of Bengal, 1732-1809. (HSLD) The Impeys lived at Newick Park, Sussex, A Silhouette of the Impey family making music, by Tiberius Cavallo was sold at Bonhams in 2006.

16th or 17th. The life I have lived here has been so very methodical and retired, as to afford no incidents or varieties worth mentioning. The party which I found when I first came down, was soon reduced to what it is at present; viz. Sir E., Lady Impey and the two Miss Impeys: and this three weeks we have really had nobody to dine or spend the evening with us, excepting once, when Admiral and Mrs. Malcolm came to dinner. In hopes of seeing you soon in Town, and of seeing you well and happy, I remain,
Yours sincerely,
T. Cavallo.

(Same letter)

My dear Mrs. Rackett,
I rejoice to hear that Mr. Baker is reconciled to his daughter – and, knowing how interested you was [sic] in the welfare of that deserving young woman, I heartily congratulate you on the happy event; wishing that everything may hereafter go on prosperously with her, as well as with the whole family. When you write your next letter to her, be pleased to mention my best complimts. and my congratulations.

To the kind enquiries you are pleased to make after my health, I have the satisfaction to answer, that the cough and oppression which began to make their appearance during the short time I remained in Town vanished soon after my arrival at this place, and at present I find myself perfectly free from both; but I much doubt whether I shall long remain so when I return to town.

Sir. E. Impey has given me such another piece of French Money as I gave you, and he says his reason for bringing it, is that the representation of Buonaparte is the greatest likeness that was ever made of him. Sir E., Lady, and Miss Impey have dined with Buonaparte and his wife: but it is remarkable that he was invited on one day, and the two ladies on another day. They were all three at the drawing room when Buonaparte had the famous altercation with Ld. Wentworth[44]. They have frequently amused me with various remarkable accounts relative to the French, Buonaparte, &c. &c.[45], but of these I shall give you a specimen or two when I have the pleasure of meeting you in Town. Mean while I remain
Yours sincerely, and much Obliged
T. Cavallo

The following belongs to Mr. Rackett, but you may read it if you please.

Dear Sir
When I first began to see that I should not be able to return to Town as soon as I

44 The reference to Lord Wentworth is a clear mistake: the 'altercation' with Napoleon was between him and Lord Whitworth on 1 March 1803. It was recorded both by Napoleon himself and also in detail in *England and Napoleon in 1803* [1887] ed. Oscar Browning, Longmans Green & Co, containing the despatches of Lord Whitworth. Lord Wentworth and his family had also visited Paris, which no doubt led to the confusion in the recollection of the letter-writer.

45 Impey was in France from 1801-1804.

intended, and hearing that a gentleman was going from this place to London, I availed myself that opportunity, and sent a packet containing your two tickets, and one of Sir Elijah's tickets, for the institution, to your house in Town, there to wait for your arrival. Now I must trouble you with a commission respecting the institution[46], which I beg you will look after without the least loss of time after your return to London. The call is that Mrs. and Miss Randall wish to continue subscribers during the next year; but they will not be in town before the latter end of February, and their old tickets cannot be got at before they return for they do not recollect where they put them; and the house has been put quite out of order by the painters and paper hangers. Now what I wish to do, is to ask whether they may continue subscribers on the old establishment, without showing the old tickets; but I want to know this as soon as possible, so that if it is not to be done easily, I may have time to inform Mrs. Randall of it, and she may write about it to her friend Mrs. Barnard, before the first of January next. Don't you forget to put up in one of your boxes for London, my packet of cloths.

I have mentioned to Sir E. Impey, who is fond of gardening, that you had seen and were in expectation of having, some pease which when fresh could be eat pod and all. As he has expressed a great desire to having some of that sort, I should be much obliged to you if you could procure some seeds of the same for Sir E. During the little time I was in Town in October last, I examined my Pyrophoric bottle, and not being satisfied with the closeness of the stop cock, I myself ground it over very accurately; in consequence of which though I filled the bottle with some pyrophorus which I prepared before I came down into Dorsetshire it now performs very well and readily. Bring your bottle to Town, and I shall perform the same operation upon it. Wishing you all health and happiness.

I remain, yours sincerely,
T. Cavallo.

D-RAC/C/42. Letter from James Lind[47] to Rev. Th. Rackett.

Windsor Sunday 24th May 1807
Dear Sir,
I trouble you with the Letter to request the pleasure of seeing you here this Week. The sooner the better, as all Mr. De Luc's[48] new-Electrical-apparatus is to be sent to London in a few days. To come here to get much new electrical information, will make

46 The Royal Institution of Great Britain was founded in 1799 and granted a royal charter in 1800. It was dedicated to the exploration of scientific and mechanical experiments. It was and still is situated in Albemarle Street, Mayfair.

47 James Lind (1736-1812) physician to the royal family at Windsor. He had an interest in scientific and historical matters and corresponded with Tiberius Cavallo and Joseph Banks.

48 Probably Jean André Deluc, F.R.S. (1727-1817) who, in 1809 forwarded a paper to the Royal Society with an account of an aerial electroscope, etc. This was not published by the Royal Society, but was accepted by *Nicholson's Journal.* His dry pile was an important discovery. (HSLD)

it I hope well worth your while; your coming here for nothing, would grieve me. I will add some Royal hand writings, and do everything in my power to make the short time I shall detain you at Windsor agreeable; and I flatter myself instructing to you, and that it will open a new field to you in electricity whether De Luc's Hypothesis is true or not, I make no doubt of.

You will please inform, us the day prior to your coming that I may be at home to receive you, and have your apartment in order: Lucy and Dorothea write in best regards, and sincere wishes to see you. I am,
Dear Sir,
Yours & most faithfully
James Lind

D-RAC/E/105. Letter from T. Cavallo to Dorothea Rackett.

Newick Park, January the 28th, 1808
My dear Dorothea,
I am much obliged to you for the various articles of information, and specimens of dyeing, contained in your two letters, which are rendered more valuable by the circumstance of their being written amongst the pleasures, the occupations, and the dissipations of London. So, notwithstanding the dullness, and bad weather, that predominated before Christmas, you contrived to creep to a ball at Blandford. I rejoice, however, to find that you could not obtain a partner to dance with; for thus you avoided catching cold, spraining your ankle, tearing your cloths, &c. &c.

I hope the Farquharsons[49] were very well when you left Dorsetshire. But you forgot to say anything of other friends, such as Lady B., my relation Lady E; and the Revd. Flug Pug. I wonder that you have not yet succeeded in your trials to make transparent paper with Canada Balsom[50]. When in Town, I showed Mrs. Windsor the manner of making it, and she has not only succeeded very readily; but is likewise much pleased with it. About a fortnight ago she sent me two very pretty landscapes painted in colour upon such paper. It is most probable, however, that by this time you have seen her, and that she may have shown you something of the sort. Though, as you say, the manufactury of hats of deal shavings is grown very common, your specimens are very beautiful, and I think the manufacture may be applied to other uses. What think you of making work baskets and work boxes of it, which might be strengthened by means of wire concealed between the plaits?

With respect to this part of the world I have hardly gone out of the grounds, and not frequently out of the house; the weather, the swamping of the ground, the bad state of the roads, and the colds and coughs I have had, having all conspired to keep me quiet at home and on mornings always in my room amongst books and

49 The Farquharson family lived at Langton Long Blandford and Eastbury, Tarrant Gunville. They were noted as early promoters of hunting and for breeding hunting dogs.
50 Canada Balsom, or Turpentine – *Terebinthina Canadensis* B.P.C. (HSLD)

papers, as you well know. In my few excursions in the environs of this house I have not met with any natural curiosities worth sending to you, excepting some seeds of what the Gardener calls Indian-shot, a little packet of which you will find in the same packet which is to contain this letter. Those seeds being remarkably sound, black and hard, I think would prove an addition to your sea weed necklace, by intermixing them with the sea weed berries. If they are too hard for you to pierce, I can get them pierced for you when I return to Town.

I am very sorry that they are few; but I had all that grew in the hothouse, excepting about half a dozen, which were kept for sowing next year. Though I have been so solitary at this place; yet some balls have been given in the neighbourhood. The Ladies of this house have been twice to the Lewes balls, and once to the Brighton ball, which was given in honour of the Queen's birthday; but it may afford some comfort to you, to hear, that, on account of a superabundance of Ladies at Brighton, one of the Miss Impeys danced two dances only, and the other could not dance at all. A ball was also given in this house, but it was a rustic one, the company consisting of the park servants, household servants, gardeners, game-keeper, butcher, &c. They had a very plentiful supper, drew King and Queen (for it was twelfth night) and danced till half past five in the morning.

Your playhouse fever, I suppose, is now at its height and your pulse must beat at least 120 whenever Mrs. Garrick[51] opens her mouth. I hear you have had a handsome dinner at their house, and met some of her husband's relations, but I am afraid there was not our friend of Drury Lane play house.

When you have dyed or spoiled the gown you intended to dye, be pleased to inform me of your success. I hope however to hear from you soon independently of that affair, and tell me everything that you have heard, seen, done, or imagined. It is now almost dark, and I expect at every moment to hear the dinner bell. I shall keep, therefore this letter open till tomorrow; for, the person who is to take my parcel to Town, does not set off before next Saturday morning.

Jan. 29th. I forgot to say that some time ago I made several trials with sulphate of iron, by exposing it in pipes to several degrees of heat, and mixing it with various salts; but I could not succeed to obtain any other colours besides the gradations between black and the usual red which you well know. Some time ago Miss Randall expressed a wish of dyeing a gown of a red colour. I wish therefore that when you see her, you will show her such another specimen as you sent me, and if she likes the colour, tell her how to make it.

I remain, My Dear Dorothea,
Yours sincerely,
T. Cavallo.

51 Eva Maria Veigel (1724 -1822, a Viennese dancer whom David Garrick married in 1749. The marriage was childless, but famously happy. After Garrick's death in 1779 she lived at the villa at Hampton which he built for them. She is buried in Westminster Abbey with her husband.

D-RAC/J/146. Letter from Rev. T. Rackett to Tiberius Cavallo.

March 3rd 1808
Dear Sir
In the first place let me thank you for the shells you were so good as to procure, which came very safe, & are very good specimens, they will do very well for my cabinet & unless you perceive any that appear to be of a different sort or shape I need not trouble you for more of them. You have seen in the Papers an account of the terrible fire which has consumed Mr. Nicholl's Printing Office and Warehouses[52]. The whole Impression of the History of Leicestershire, the work of many years and the last volume nearly printed of the History of Dorset have been consumed and his loss, (as he was only insured for a very small amount) is very considerable. But the copper plates, &c. are safe so that the History of Dorset will be reprinted. His friend Mr. Gough who had been ill & was got pretty well, has been much impaired that it is feared he will never be himself again.

We have heard lately from the Archdeacon of Dorset[53] who enquires after you and appears to be in good health and spirits. I have seen Mr. Prado, and Dr. Bancroft Junr. who both desired to be remembered to you.

We had on Thursday last a Paper at the Royal Society giving an account of an extensive apparatus for the production of gaslights in a Cotton Manufactory at Manchester by the person who first produced the effect for Messrs. Bolton & Watt[54]. This apparatus is on a more extensive scale so that the tubes convey the gas a distance of several miles. The lights produced are equal to those of upwards of 2000 candles, and by calculating the expences attending the support of such a light with Tallow candles would be upwards of £2000 per ann. (if burnt 3 hours every day). The expence of gas lights after deducting for the Coke &c. is £600 only. The apparatus answers perfectly, there is no bad smell, and the House of the Proprietor is completely lighted in the same beautifull way, but you will observe that all this is performed in a Country where Coal is to be had at the cheapest rate, so that it will never become a general practice, nor is it desirable that the consumption of coal should be greatly increased.

There is a Perpetual Motion now exhibiting, the appearance of which is here represented, An ivory Ball D is suspended by a watch spring C, and swings in a Glass vessel from A. to B. a space of about 8 inches. It will immediately occur to you that the ball is put in motion by a stream of air from the orifice of the Glass vessel E and

52 John Nichols (1745-1826) printer, publisher and antiquarian. His *History and Antiquities of the County of Leicestershire*, published in four volumes between 1795 and 1815, was one of the most ambitious of the county histories. He was co-author of the first complete publication of Domesday Book in 1783. He was Editor of the *Gentleman's Magazine* from 1788 until his death. His printing works in Fleet Street suffered a catastrophic fire in 1808, in which the proofs for most of the 2nd edition of Hutchin's *History of Dorset* were lost.

53 In 1808 the Archdeacon of Dorset was Henry Hall (1734-1815), rector of Child Okeford 1758-1815 and Archdeacon 1801 until his death.

54 William Murdock pioneered a method of gas-lighting using coal-gas, which he developed further when he joined the Birmingham firm of Boulton and Watt. He installed experimental gas lights in their Soho works and in 1806 the cotton spinning mill of Phillips and Lee was illuminated by his gas lamps, the first installation of gas lighting in the country.

7 Drawing of Perpetual Motion machine by Thomas Rackett [D-RAC/J/146]

consequently that when the external air and the air in the room are of the same temperature there will be no stream at all. The Proprietor however asserts that the Ball is put in motion notwithstanding such change of temperature, and that the contrivance is a very simple one.

The motion of the Pendulum is sufficient to give motion to the Wheels of a clock which may be applied at C. But I leave you to pronounce how far you believe it possible for a stream of air to proceed constantly from the orifice & in what manner it is effected.

Mr. Davy[55] is so well recovered from his late illness that he is to resume his office at the Institution and to begin his lectures of Electric-Galvanic Influence in the course of next week.

I have procured the Transactions have sent one to Dr. Lind as you desired.
I hope you are quite free from Colds and that the weather will shortly admit of your coming to London; But I think you perfectly right to stay in the Country till Winter has left us. I remain Dear Sir Yours sincerely
T.R.

D-RAC/E/107. John Knowles of the Navy Office, Biographer of Fuseli, to the Revd. Thomas Rackett.

Revd. Dear Sir,
I have taken the liberty of sending by this night's post the courier newspaper which gives an account of the operations of our army (and most probably the last) in Spain. I regard the fall of Sir John Moore[56], as a great misfortune to the country, the loss of such a general in the present dearth of military talents is much to be deplored and most certainly not to be retrieved; with a great degree of personal courage, he united coolness and decision, his late retreat has marked his professional character, perhaps more than his victory. He was the idol of the soldiery, but the dread of the officers, or at least of those who are fit only for Bond Street or Brooks's, with all his professional knowledge, he had a mind formed for, and cultivated by elegant and useful knowledge.

Such is the man whose loss we deplore, and such I have long known him to be by the support of a friend (Mr. Fuseli) who hides no faults, but discovers all blemishes. Mr. F. has to deplore the loss of a friend and a companion. I called at your house last week, the servant mentioned that there were no letters but the private ones from the Royal Institute.The weather in this part of the country has been for the last week, most unpleasant; the fall of snow has been so great that the carriages move along the streets with some difficulty; I have experienced more inconvenience from a cold this winter than during any preceeding one, but by dint of a pretty strong constitution, my health is now much better. I hope Mrs. Rackett is recovering from her late indisposition.

---

55 Humphry Davy, (1778-1829), chemist and inventor. He successfully separated chemical elements using electricity. On the opening of the Royal Institution in 1799, Davy was appointed Assistant Lecturer, becoming Director and Principal Lecturer shortly afterwards. His lectures on electricity and galvanism, often involving spectacular experiments, attracted large audiences. He is now chiefly remembered for his Davy lamp, an early form of arc light.

56 Lt. Gen. Sir John Moore (1761-1809), died fighting courageously at the Battle of Corunna during the Peninsular War. He undertook much-needed reforms in the British Army.

I attend a lecture at the Royal Academy this evening, delivered by Mr. Carlisle, the lecturer of Anatomy, he has given the academicians sufficient reasons to expect much from him; during the present unfavourable weather we cannot expect you in London, but will it not be right to be ready for your departure from the country, so as to be enabled to take advantage of the first favourable opportunity.

All the family in Titchfield street are well, except the Countess, and it is likely that her health will not be very strong till she presents her husband with an addition to his family. I beg you will present my respectful compliments to Mrs. and Miss Rackett. I have this instant received a sermon with the Editor's compliments, I enquired who was the editor and I understand that his name is Webb and a resident near Poole, Dorsetshire, I therefore apprehend that I am indebted to you for this present, I perceive too that it is on a subject that concerns a young man " marriage" perhaps Secker[57] may put the question in a new light, but I really think that he can tell me nothing on that subject which I have not thought, however, I will give it a speedy perusal, and will shortly give you my opinion of its merits. Mr. King desires his best compts. to you and your family – I am Revd. Dear Sir
Your devoted
And obedt. Servt.
John Knowles.
Navy Office
23 Janr. 1809

D-RAC/E/104. Letter from Mrs. E. Pulteney[58] to Dorothea Rackett.

Queen Square, Nov. 19. 1810
My dear Dorothea,
I have been so engaged, & so employed, & circumstanced that I could not write to you at my ease, & since that time, I thought your wished return so near approaching, that I judged it scarcely worth while; but an event has just occur'd in which I think you will feel yourself so deeply interested, that I cannot forbear to condole with you – it is nothing less than the demolition of Vauxhall[59]! that enchanting scene, so long the delight of the young & the gay! nor were its powers of pleasing confined to those; witness Mrs Garrick & myself who last year enjoyed in a new light, & am sure increased splendour, a place of resort which was in the days of our youth rural, tho highly embellished, and perhaps not less charming than of late, when it was rendered the Temple of Fame: & by its brilliancy, & various accommodations, compensated in

57 Probably Thomas Secker (1693-1768), Archbishop of Canterbury. (HSLD)
58 Elizabeth, née Galton (1739-1820) widow of Dr. Richard Pulteney (1730-1801). Her husband trained at Edinburgh as an apothecary and physician. He acted as physician to his distant cousin Sir William Pulteney of Bath until the latter's death in 1764, after which he moved to Blandford. *A Catalogue of the Birds, Shells and Some of the more Rare Plants of Dorsetshire, illustrated,* by Richard Pulteney and Thomas Rackett was published by Nichols in 1813
59 Vauxhall Gardens, on the south bank of the Thames, first developed in 1785.

some measure for the loss of Ranelagh[60]; another scene which in my juvenile days I could not have imagined would ever have been deserted; as nothing could be more exhilarating & delightful to every sense. All, all is gone! The assembly of Heroes dispersed & like the "baseless fabric of a vision", not a wreck is left behind[61], to say this once was dear Vauxhall! I remember a pretty song, which when I was a Child was sung in all companies.

> Oh Mary soft in feature
> I've been at dear Vauxhall,
> No Paradise is sweeter
> Nor that they Eden call
> At night such new vagaries
> Such gay and harmless sport,
> All looked like Giant-fairies
> And this their Monarch's Court,
> The man of the Moon twear'd slily
> As tho' 'twould please him highly
> To taste delights like these[62].

This is all I can recollect of it, & enough; as I dare say your Mama knows it well, & will shew it you among her old songs. I well knew that I had seen it for the last time, but I little thought I should survive, & <u>thus</u> lament it! I thought the powerful duty <u>interest</u> would have preserved it, for the receipts must have been great. We may say, "The taste of pleasure now is o'er",[63] for what amusement is there now that can be compared with it? I hope though, how deeply soever you may feel this stroke, it will not deter you from coming to Town. This smoky, foggy, filthy place may still afford some attractions for you, you may find gratification in such fare as the Royal Institution yet affords, in Chemistry, Galvanism, &c. but I am so deprived of all my delights in it, that I have determined not to subscribe to it this year. Not that I knew whether it is in existence. We used before this time to have the meetings (and the Lecturers) announced, & indeed commend but nothing transpires. Before I went into the country, I heard Mr. Watson say, I must be in Town on such a day, as there is hope of a meeting of the Proprietors of the Institution, but ere this it may be defunct.

It is time to say I received with great pleasure your kind and agreeable Club-letter soon after my arrival in Rutlandshire, whither I went unaccompanied, for we are become too numerous now to go in a body to any moderate house. We have been

60 Ranelagh Gardens, Chelsea, opened in 1742.

61 A slight misquotation from *The Tempest* IV.1.154-56, following the version on Shakespeare's 1741 monument in Westminster Abbey, rather than his original lines.

62 Composed by English composer Thomas Gladwin (1710-1799), words by John Lockman (fl. 1730s).

63 From *Arno's Vale*, reputedly by Charles Sackville, Earl of Middlesex, written at Florence c.1737, addressed to his mistress, Signora Muscovita, a singer.

therefore a divided family. With me Mr. Basketts family i.e. himself, his wife and two little Girls, filled Mrs. Foster's spare rooms for six weeks. My visits *en passant* were only a rest of a few days, going & returning, as Mrs. Hodson was not well, and the Duberlys all on a ramble to the Lakes &c. Mary spent most of the time of my absence at Mr. J. St. Barbes[64] at Winchmere Hill (ten miles out of town) with little Charles & the Baby, & sometimes her Husband George was sent to Lymington to bathe in hopes his eyes might be benefitted, but they stand just as they did.

In the shooting season Mr. St. B. passed six weeks at Lymington, and now we are all together again. Our little Girl is all vivacity & good humour & I think you will like her as well as any Miss of her age. Her eyes are remarkably dark, and bright, & it is thought she will excel her Mother in brownness. I hope she will have roses to set off the nut-brown tincture of her skin. After my return, I had a bad cold, with the worst cough I have ever experienced; it has left me deaf in one ear (an evil of which I shall be more sensible when you arrive if I cannot get rid of it) and apparently ten years older than when we parted. The rest of the family are in good plight.

Mr. St. Barbe's sister has been with us for three weeks, & has taken up much of our time in making preparations for her Nuptials, which are to take place at Lymington on the 27th instant. Her swain is a young Surgeon of the name of Coombe nephew to the Alderman, & one of thirteen children; two of them were lately married in one day, & a third about a week before. They are to be our neighbours a little beyond the British Museum. I have no tidings yet to send you of our Persian friends, but John Morier[65] is safely arrived in America; I wish he may be able to manage those tough people better than any Agents we have sent thither hitherto. We are (as I think all must be) anxious for the recovery of our good Sovereign[66]. That unfortunate King is believed to be the cause of the sad disaster; the attendants feared the consequences, but were unable to refuse the request of the poor dying sufferer, he was certainly much & immediately affected by it.

As Antiquarians, you must have been attentive to the late discoveries in St. George's Chapel[67] a Gentleman with whom I am somewhat acquainted, says the eyes of both Mother and Child are brilliant, & that he touched the lips of the later, to

64 Mrs. Pulteney's niece married into the St. Barbe family

65 John Morier (1766-1853), diplomat. In 1810 he was sent as Secretary to the Legation at Washington DC.

66 George III, already ill and almost blind from cataracts, had a serious relapse in 1810, brought on by the death of his youngest and favourite daughter, Princess Amelia from tuberculosis. A Regency was established which lasted until the King's death in 1820.

67 The "Royal Vault" beneath St. George's Chapel in Windsor was excavated between 1804 and 1810 on the instructions of King George III. During subsequent work under the Chapel Quire, workmen accidentally broke through a wall of the vault of King Henry VIII, and it was noted that this also held two additional coffins plus a child's mahogany coffin. One contained the remains of Charles I, opened on 1 April 1813 with the Prince Regent's permission. The royal physician Sir Henry Halford was at pains to note that the coffin of Queen Jane Seymour was not touched. The coffin of Henry VIII was noted as damaged with his skeleton visible. The smallest coffin contained a still-born child of Queen Anne. A marble slab in the centre of St George's Quire now records the identity of all four in the vault beneath.

see the teeth, & found them elastic. How much of this you will find credible I know not; but having heard what you said on seeing the Sarcophagus of Alexander, it is a question among us whether you would not like to form a trio with those good people, & be closed up with them in this same excellent pickle, such another opportunity may never again occur, but if you have any thought of it, let me enquire whether a place may not be secured for you some seventy or eighty years hence, I suppose the pickle may then be equally good, and indeed we cannot spare you at present.

As many of your old neighbours are leaving you, and some of the new ones do not turn out exactly what you could wish, I rejoice to hear that you have some such as may be worthy of your acquaintance. We are to visit the Moriers this evening, & I will speak of Mr. and Mrs. Raikes. I cannot tell who Lady Mildmay was, or how connected with Dorsetshire.

I think Sir W. O. should have made beauty an object in the choice of a wife, for certainly he has none of his own to impart to his family. I am sorry you had any trouble in calling on Mrs. Baskett, she I find has been rambling most of the summer.

If Mr. Rackett can contrive to send all or any of my Plants, and Box, to Poole, so that they may travel in good company with his own moveables, I will thank him, and gladly pay any expence he may incur in the business. Have you not been and paddling in the dirt at Charlton? Surely you will not be less interested in the curiosities produced in your own ground, than in that of others. I am glad to hear you have had such success among the Fungi. I found one which had it been fresh, I thought might have been worthy of your attention, as it is, I have brought it home, and we will talk of it togeth. Apropos' in return for Mr. Rackett's Tode (with whose name I am well acquainted) and his tanning skinner, I desire him to accept Mr. Patten (a gentleman known to this family) who married Miss Clogg. & Mrs. J. St. Barbes observation was, "it was very easy to convert Miss Clogg into a Patten, she only wanted a Ring". We shall have great antiquarian conferences when we meet. Friday, We passed an agreeable evening with the female Moriers. Mrs. M. says she knows Mr. Raikes family well, they are amiable, well informed, and that his Father is so opulent a merchant that tho' he has a large family, he gave his Daughters £30,000 each.

You will perhaps not receive this letter so early as the date will indicate, but I could not make you pay for all this odd stuff.

"Laugh they who win." say I.

Safely arrived in Q. Square, a basket containing a Chick-eyne, Cathead apples, and Swan-egg Pears, for which due thanks are returned. And there will be people found who will have the hardihood to eat them without fear. The Pears we can already say are excellent.

As in these days I suspect there are not many St. Barbes to be cut off, I feel no horror at the sight of a razor, but wish it was more employed; for I have long complained that the beard is making frightful inroads on the face. When Miss. R. Writes enigmas, she should be careful not to render them doubly puzzling by the omission of a word, it required all My sagacity to find a Rhyme to Daughter. Slaughter is the most perfect rhyme, but palter serves best perhaps for meaning.

On Sunday last Dorothea should have received a letter, that whenever it arrives, ought to make her feel much compunction for all the bitter invectives she has poured forth against her nice Friend.

All the enigmas being solved by F.P. before Christmas, she demands the price of three letters (I am very moderate in saying twelve) without delay, from the propounders. If they fail, may one of them never have another Lover & the other two never have the gratification of tasting a P-lover-egg while they live!!! After these terrible denunciations, I trust you will all take to your Pens to avert the impending evils.

Soldiers in Peace and Chimneys in Summer, are equally useless. If there is any hidden meaning in it, there it must still lie for me.

My 'eyne' do not pretend to penetrate to the center of a Millstone nor even through an Eggshell, but my tongue had the sagacity to eject the monster instead of swallowing him (no, I would rather swallow a lobster (piece-meal) than either serpent or Crocodile) as you shall be convinced when you come to Town, for tho' I do not enter the list against the anonymous antagonist who pronounces it a Chicken, unsight, unseen. I shall not yield to this sentence, till it is confirmed by the learned who shall see it. It must be allowed that the race alluded to, have subdued all the Monsters that came before them, what greater boast can St. George make?

As to the letter S. he has so long been the disgrace of our language that I could not have supposed that three great Musicians, like my Friends at Spetisbury, would have been his advocate; but rather that they would have consigned him to the sole use of the Serpent tribe. For I observe that he is always smothered by the vocal Cognoscenti. Those who wear a collar of S.S. might be expected to stand forth as his Champions, but they, tho' mighty, are not numerous.

No my own Sweet Dorothea, I will not believe, tho' I have it under your own hand that you are such a revengeful little gipsy. Nor that you are so wicked as to resolve to do evil that good may come. No, you will not deny that virtue is its own reward, tho' sometimes we are apt to lay claim to some other reward, & complain that it is long in coming. What can you say worse of me now, than that I am better than my word? I know your next letter will be written in a very different strain & after assuring you that we all lament that there is no immediate prospect of seeing you in Town, I shall bid you all adieu and resign my Pen to Mary. My good Friends, Believe me
Ever Yours. E. Pulteney.
Q. Square. Nov. 24th 1810

The other day I saw from the carriage a Foreigner in a yellow silk dress with fine fringe and a handsome Turban, a very elegant Gentleman was walking with him. Little Charles exclaimed, why that is the Persa Abassada! He must have judged from your drawing, for he never saw him. To prove to you how perfectly good-natured I am, tho' you say you withheld from us much interesting & amusing intelligence, I inform you that your favorite The Mirza arrived safely at Malta, but it will be many months ere we shall learn that he is actually in Persia. You may have some curiosity to know what is become of the Marquis. After long delays at Malta, &c. we learn that he is now in Smyrna. I fancy the meeting could not be very cordial between him and his family. Mr.

St. B. had one interview with his Brother. We have reason to believe they are a pair of Brothers.

D-RAC/C/47. Letter from An Exhibitor of Natural phenomena, From a friends house in Queen Square.

14 Jany. 1811.
The Exhibitor hopes for the honour of Mr. Racketts patronage as he is an admirer of Natural phee nomona [sic][68]. The Exhibitor begs leave to add that the monster was first shewn in Foster Lane, & will shortly be removed to Barbican, of which however due notice will be given.

Foot note by C. St. Barbe reads:-"Some persons not conversant with geography have doubted whether such a place exists as Heneaga; Mr. Rackett need not be told that it is one of the Bahama Islands."

[The Exhibitor's card reads]

To be seen
At No. 26. Queen Square
A MOST WONDERFUL NONDESCRIPT MONSTER
Supposed to be a Native of Heneaga.
Also lately arrived
The Celebrated Barbary Venus
Who cannot speak a word of English
Nearly approaching the Hottentot Venus in Colour
Her Parents are said to be Natives of Alljeers.

D-RAC/E/107. John Knowles[69] of the Navy Office to Revd. Th. Rackett.

Revd. Dear Sir,
The enclosed letter came to your house yesterday. Mr. Sowerby has returned from Plymouth and on his way visited Portsmouth Dockyard, he informs me that dry rot is not confined to the *Queen Charlotte*, as he saw a 74 Gunship at Portsmth. in quite as bad a state, this is truly alarming; among a number of fungi of inferior note, now flourishing on the timber removed from the *Charlotte*, he has selected the following which have overspread the ship. Viz: *Boletus hybridus* Eng. Fungi Tab. 289. *Boletus Medulla panis* E.F. 326. *Xylostrom a giganteum* E. F. 358. *Auricularia pulverulenta* E.F. 214. *Boletus Lachrymans* E.F. 113; but the latter was not very abundant. The degree

68 For phee nomona we should read phenomena. (HSLD)

69 Knowles worked in the surveyor's department of the Navy Office, publishing several works on naval matters. He was elected a Fellow of the Royal Society for his scientific researches, and was an original member of the Athenæum Club.

of moisture was very great, an hygrometer whose scale of perfect wet is 100[70], stood outside of the ship at 464 degrees but placed in the hold it was at 828 degrees, Mr. Sowerby recommends that the ship should be dried by a circulation of atmospheric air, and not by stoves as has been usual.

The affair in Spain and (for a time only I fear) prosperous; but we have no account from Russia. As I have received the proof sheets of the history of Dorsetshire, they have been sent to Mr. Nicholls. I understand that the Rev. Mr. Tattersall has called at your house and that he is in good health. Hammond has got the picture but I desire him not to take it to King Street until your return, as damp air will kill vanish recently put upon a picture. Davy's work is not yet published he discovered an error and it was necessary to cancel one of the sheets. I understand that his attention is so much given to Lady Davy, that his Booksellers cannot get him to write a letter. The mention that you made of a journey to Milton Abbey, awakened in my mind the recollection of a trip thither with you, the delightful prospect from the eminence around the house, the collection of pictures, the gothic abbey, but above all the pleasant company that I enjoyed that day, cannot be forgotten. I cannot say that I have very much of envy in my composition, but yet wished to have been by your side on your late excursion. I should have written to you some days back, but I have been much engaged in difficult calculations. Government are about to establish a fund for the widows and children of such clerks as may die while they belong to this office, and we are to ascertain how much money it will require for that purpose; I could but lend my aid to further so desirable an object. I beg that you will make my respectful compliments to Mrs. and Miss Rackett, tell the latter that Drury Lane theatre is very nearly finished except the painters work. I am with truth Rev. Dr. Sir,
Yours J. Knowles.
7 Aug. 1812

D-RAC/C/52. Sir Richard Hoare of Stourhead[71] to Rev. Th. Rackett. No date (c. 1815). From Mere.

Dear Sir,
My intended Roman Progress is as follows. Wednesday 16th To trace the Roman Road from Sarum to Woodyates – Thursday17th from Woodyates to Badbury Rings examine the camp to see if our Survey is correct – sleep at Blandford. Friday 18th I am

70 This is written as1000 in Dewar's original text, which would agree with the other readings, but corrected by him to 100 in his *Errata.* John Knowles was something of an expert in this area. He was Secretary of the Committee of Surveyors of the Navy, and in 1821 he was to publish a work on the *Means to be taken to Preserve the British Navy from Dry Rot.*

71 Sir Richard Colt Hoare (1758-1838) of Stourhead, antiquary and archaeologist, came from a wealthy family, but took over his large estate at the age of 25 on condition that he left the family banking business (which remains the UK's oldest privately owned bank). After some foreign travel he became increasingly interested in local antiquities. His publication, *Ancient History of North and South Wiltshire* came out in stages between 1812 and1819.

at your service and will be with you before eleven when we can take our antiquarian ride – and I will partake of your family dinner – my Surveyor will be employed on that day at Hambledon Hill. I am also at liberty on Saturday for a ride to Comb ditch, etc.

On the 20th I am engaged to my friend Mr. Davis at Turnworth[72]. A line forwarded to The Greyhound Inn will find me. These are my plans, health and weather not preventing. If the day is fine on Thursday you may perhaps join us at Badbury about the middle of the day[73].

I am, Dear Sir
Truly yours
Richd. C. Hoare.

D-RAC/C/52. Letter from Sir Richard Colt Hoare to the Rev. Th. Rackett. From Stourhead. 23 Jan. 1818.

My dear Sir
Your very gratifying letter deserves my earliest acknowledgement. I had heard of the discovery – but knew not its merit – which your sketch has developed – there certain was a *Via Romana* from Ilchester to Dorchester, which led near the place of this discovery – and I am very happy to hear that Lord Ilchester has taken means to preserve it – I have long promised him a visit and this will be a gratifying sight and I shall endeavour to persuade him to investigate the ground thoroughly. Many thanks for the list of Bridges on the Stour – I suppose you will shortly think of changing your quarters – Lambert[74] is in high spirits having seen both the Humboldt and expecting daily another envoye of <u>Aridities</u> from Spain he has lately flowered at Boyton a <u>Vonder</u> from Peru. With best compliments to your Ladies, believe me, Dear Sir,
Very sincerely yours
R.C. Hoare.

D-RAC/C/52. Sir Richard Colt Hoare to Rev. Th. Rackett.

Stourhead 25th Sept. [no date]
Dear Sir,
I think I shall visit the neighbourhood of Blandford upon antiquarian business some

72 Mark Davis (d. 1832), a Bristol merchant who also had a seat at Holnest near Sherborne. He built Turnworth House in about 1800. It was burnt down after the second World War.

73 H.S.L. Dewar discovered letters from Rackett to Charles Hatchett about the discovery of a Roman Chariot on Hamdon Hill in 1817, which he wrote up in *Somerset and Dorset Notes and Queries*, Vol. XXIX, Pt. 288, September 1968, Pp. 36-38.

74 A.B. Lambert F.R.S. 1761-1842. Lived at Boyton House near Heytesbury in Wilts. Where he started his own private museum and herbarium before he was old enough to go to school. (HSLD)

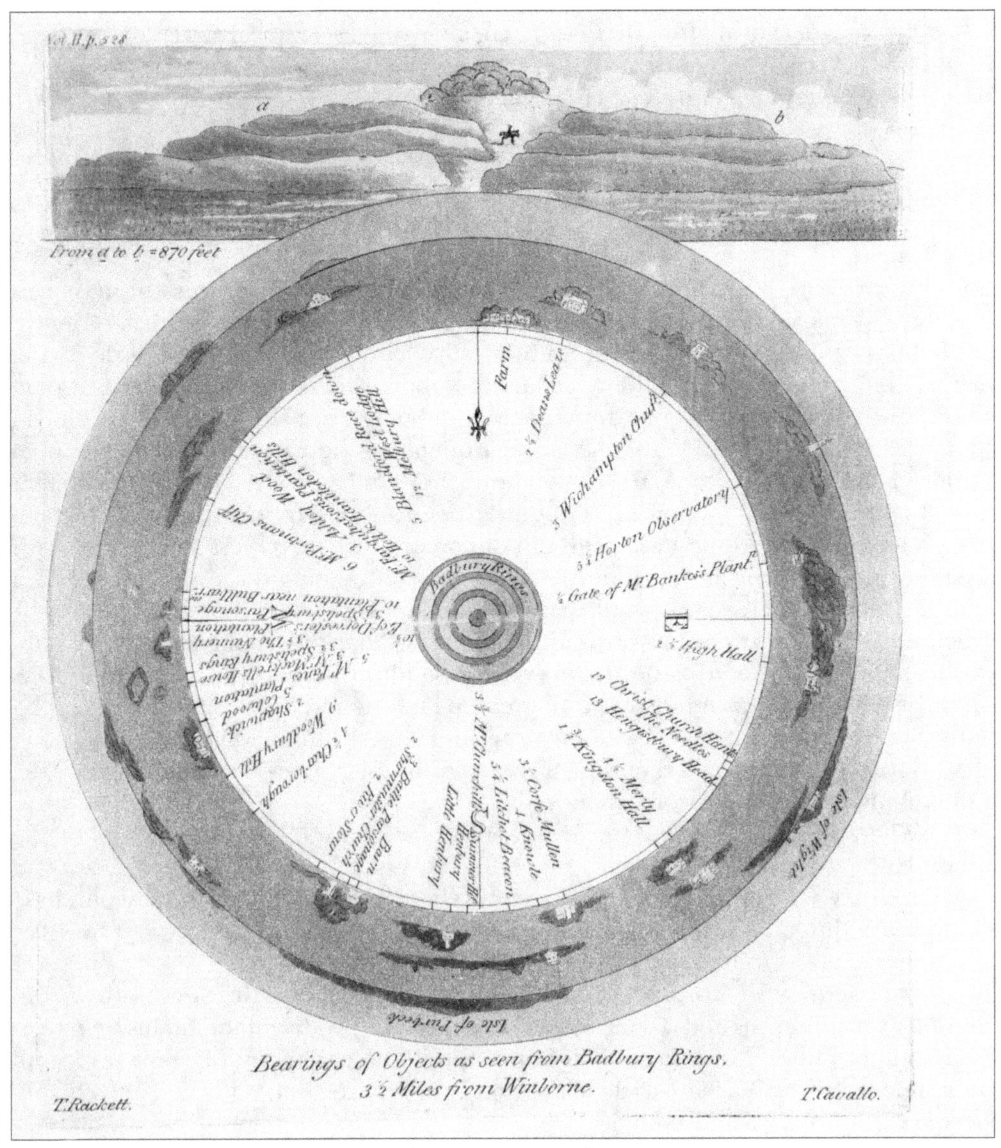

8 Bearings of Objects from Badbury Rings, drawn by Thomas Rackett and Tiberius Cavallo (Hutchins, History of Dorset, *2nd edition, vol. ii, p. 256)*

time between the 15th and 20th and should you then be resident at Spettisbury[75], I shall be happy to pay my respects to you and take a ride on the Ikenield [sic] Street with you. Our friend Lambert left me this morning in high health and spirits not a little

75 The accepted modern spelling is Spetisbury. The name has been transcribed as written in the original letters.

elated by the safe arrival of his *hortus siccus* from Madagascar and Peru.
I am, Dear Sir,
Your most obedient Servant, R.C. Hoare.

D-RAC/E/107. John Knowles to Mrs. Rackett.

Dear Madam,
The close of every year causes considerable business in all public offices, this has been the case with me, and prevented me from paying the respect due to my private friends.

I have very recently had very communicative letters from the Countess de Barde, they still remain in the South of France and live upon what is there called a handsome income a trifle under £500 per annum; the Chevalier[76] is made principal painter in Natural History to Louis the 18th, he has apartments in the Palace and a small annual income, he sold his pictures to the King for one thousand guineas, it is to be hoped that he will take care of his money; he is not an expensive but a thoughtless man. I was in great hopes that you would have been in London ere this; the Opera has opened with a very strong Company and with prospects of the season being successful, Miss O'Neil attracts as much as ever and Kean[77] has just played a character (Sir Giles Overreach) which has equally surprised as pleased the Town, so that the public amusements are worth attending to. We bring out (I say we because I have paid a little attention to it) A *Midsummer Night's Dream* tomorrow, with great splendour and the whole strength of the house at Covent Garden which, with the music by Handel, I think will be very successful.

I have frequently called in King Street, your house and everything there are safe, and nothing has occurred worth mentioning.

When Miss Rackett comes to London, she shall have the Rembrant [sic] or the Vandyck which I have, to study from, the latter Mr Ottley[78] thinks excellent. Have you seen Dr. Henry's[79] last Edition of his work upon a bare inspection that I made a purchase of it, I really think it is the best book upon science that I have seen, I do not however pretend to judge of its merit as a book on chemistry.

At length, after Lord Elgin has for years denied being in possession of Mr. Twedell's[80] manuscripts and drawings on Greece, he has produced them, this we owe to the Edinburgh Review who treated his Lordship with no ceremony. I beg my respectful compliments to Miss Rackett, and believe that I am with respect,
Dear Madam, Your very devoted St.

76 Chevalier de Barde (1777–1828) was Vicomte Alexandre-Isidore Leroy de Barde, a self-taught French painter in watercolour, who fled to England in 1792 to escape the Revolution. He exhibited several times at the Royal Academy, where some of his paintings remain. In 1817 King Louis XVIII acquired from him six large gouaches, which are now in the Louvre.

77 E. Kean, 1787-1833, Shakespearean actor. (HSLD)

78 W.Y. Ottley, writer on fine arts, 1771-1836. (HSLD)

79 William Henry, 1774-1836. (HSLD) Chemist with a particular interest in gases. His *Elements of Experimental Chemistry* (1799) was very popular, going through eleven editions.

80 John Twedell, 1769-1799. (HSLD) Classical scholar and writer.

J. Knowles.
Navy Office, 16 Jan. 1816.

D-RAC/C/52. Sir Richard Colt Hoare to Rev. Th. Rackett.

Dawlish, Devon, 18 Feb. 1816.
Dear Sir,
Every additional information respecting the antiquities of our Island is truly acceptable to me, and I beg leave to return my thanks to you for the communications contained in your letter of 30th January. I made a short excursion during the last summer into Dorsetshire and chiefly with a view to survey the many fine Camps with which that county abounds. My Surveyor Mr. Crocker completed Maiden Castle, Badbury, Hod Hill – and has others in view – particularly Hamilton [sic] Hill adjoining Hod – which is one of the grandest Earthworks I ever beheld. Neither did the Camp at Milbourne[81] escape our notice: in many respects it bears the form adopted by the Roman but the entrance appears to have been made by the Saxons. It lies very much in the line of the Roman road which I have traced very satisfactorily from Sarum to Badbury rings where there is a singularity worthy your notice whenever you are on the spot – on following the track of the ancient .... from Critchell, just as you come to the foot of the hill on which the earthwork stands you will plainly perceive two diverging causeways. A is the road to Durnovaria or Dorchester – and B seems to point in a line towards Wareham and has evidently been covered by the subsequent ramparts of the Camp. Hutchins has not mentioned this circumstance - nor have we any information of a Roman road tending to Wareham. This would be a useful discovery. I saw a great portion of another *via* which led from Hamworthy near Poole probably to the station of Vindogladia on Gussage Cow down[82]. I think the works at Charlton are probably British – or attached to some settlement of the Romanized Britons, as you mention having found pottery in the neighbourhood. The banks etc. also seem to indicate some neighbouring settlement. I think Dorsetshire if minutely investigated would prove equally fertile in British remains, with Wiltshire – When I next visit the neighbourhood of Blandford I shall think myself fortunate in finding you at home and visiting these interesting places with you.

My labours amongst the Britons in North Wiltshire are nearly completed and ready for the bookseller – I shall be always happy to hear of any new discovery you may make in the field of antiquity. I return to Stourhead next week.
I am, Dear Sir,
Your obedient Servant,
Richd. C. Hoare.

81 Known as Weatherbury Castle, a small multivallate hillfort in the parish of Milborne St Andrew, which also encloses a brick obelisk erected in 1761 by Edmund Morton Pleydell.
82 Vindogladia (or Vindocladia or Bindoclada) has been placed at many sites, from Badbury Rings to Wimborne Minster. Since 2013 excavations by Martin Papworth of the National Trust have identified it at Shapwick, Dorset.

D-RAC/D/86. Letter from George Baker, Barrister, to Mrs. Rackett.

My dear Aunt,
I am just come to Town & shod. have expected to find you here had not my sister in law Fanny Andrews told me that she passed you on the Western road about ten days ago. Perhaps the girls or one of them have told you that the Governor is mending apace in his paces. But I have seen so little of any of them that you must forgive me if this shod. be a Greyhound (i.e. a twice told tale). We were at Ramsgate about three weeks during which time in a truly Irish manner I was at Maidstone. Whilst we were there we were sumptuously fed with turtle venison and other good things which with other circumstances gave rise to an epigram of wh. I will favour you with a copy. In a cause then and there tried the Common Sergeant (a limb of the Corporation of London) and one of the City Counsel, and a City Attorney named Lavie were engaged. I need not remind one of your extensive reading accompanied too as you are by a male and female Encyclopoedia that Augusta is the poetical name of the said city, but will instead of doing so proceed to transcribe

To come from Town Augusta sought,
But knew not how't could be;
So Turtle ven'son and good cheer
Were to transport her body here;
Her Counsel to Convey her mind,
(For that must not be left behind;)
Her limbs her Common Sergeant brought
Her life itself Lavie.

Maidstone Augt. 1816
Whilst we were at Canterbury Mrs. Siddons[83] and her daughter were staying at Dr. Martow's (a prebendary) and we had the pleasure of meeting her and hearing her read a part of Shakespeare's Play called Henry VIII. I do not think that her school is in sufficient estimation with you to enduce you to think much of this treat. But I was highly delighted with it and in return for the pleasure she gave me I let her have my boy on her lap and he was good enough to leave her quite clean and dry. When I saw Jane Wheler or Mrs. Wheler at Broadstairs she was looking very well in spite of Mr. Wheler's suspicions to the contrary. I am afraid I shall not see my uncle during this London campaign. I have found a letter from him on my table. In answer to your question what can the Boy be doing in London now? I inform you that he is here much against his inclination but as the London Sessions begin tomorrow and he is beginning to attend them he has torn himself from the bosom of his family and the delights of nature to visit this abhored den of vice and folly.

I shall not visit the Parks today for fear that my spleen may be excited by the

83 Sarah Siddons (1755-1831) née Kendle, a Welsh-born celebrity actress who specialised in maternal roles and tragedies, particularly playing the role of Hamlet over three decades.

jaded old debauchees that still hover about the scenes of their unseasonable and ridiculous dissipation. The Blandford Rans[84] were over Before Fanny went to the Glynns – and as she was too late for them and too soon for another event to make a visit to that place piquant she did not see it at all. But she visited the other repository of *soi disant* maidens in your neighbourhood & is not I believe much pleased at having her idea of a nun banished by the sight of them. She like most others had pictured to herself something too beautiful to live in the world and dangerous to society for the passions they might excite if not indulge. But alas, the danger that Society has to dread from them is as Mrs. Garrick will tell you quite of another sort. But peace be with them. They now serve to my remembrance one of the happiest summers that ever I spent and as that is the case you may tell the old souls when you see them that the recollection of them often brings to my mind a train of very pleasant thoughts. Bussey has lost an Uncle in Law Dr. Charles Taylor. He was kind to her but not so necessary to her happiness as to make his loss an affliction. Ergo she is well. Wickey is better than I have seen him for years – John is grown fat and his wife both fat & round. Her shape is about to undergo an alteration such as baloon [sic] does when a considerable portion of the air which inflates it makes its escape.

I am altogether well i.e. I & I and our progeny, this is a summary account of the family for of the Governor I have spoken above & my nephew & nieces are included in the respective heads of their families. Let this example lead you to give me as favourable an account of you three. Let me hear that you are not the worse for your journey and that Mr. R. and Dorothea have abandoned their pursuit of disturbing the bones of the dead men in their graves. If they are not cautious they will if they persevered in their misdemeanour soon find themselves before a Court of Quarter Sessions. Resurrection men[85] are more closely watched now than they have been & if they shod. be indicted it may be beyond my skill to get them off. Give my love to them & believe me to remain me dearest Aunt
Your very affectionate nephew
George Baker.

D-RAC/E/111. Letter from Thomas King, Paymaster of the 98th Regiment in Canada, to Thomas Rackett.

Frederick N.B. 8th October 1817.
My dear Friend,
Here we are again in New Brunswick and here we will remain I imagine till the reduction of the Regiment. We left Halifax in July last, Mrs. King remains there till

84 Blandford Races were held on the downs above the town from at least 1603. The area is now occupied by Blandford Military Camp, and the horse-races are remembered in the name Racedown Road.
85 Resurrection men were really body-snatchers. The Anatomy Act of 1832 largely put a stop to their practise owing to the licensing of anatomical Schools and the provision of subjects to anatomists. (HSLD)

something certain is ascertained about the Regiment. The place we are at is a neat little Village 84 miles from St. John, situate on the banks of one of the finest Rivers in this part of America. You wou'd be delighted with the present appearance of the Autumnal tints, they are so various and rich. There's a Steam Boat[86] working between this place and St. John, which conveys you from one place to the other in 14 hours. I go down monthly for money for the Regiment.

Pray have you heard of anything about Mrs Bingham at the Alms-house at Newington butts? In several of my letters I mentioned this person to you and my expectation from that quarter, but I do not recollect your having noticed it in your letters. I should like to know very much whether she is alive.

I have an uncommon large dog by name of Bran, by name, the wonder of everybody on this side of the water and intend sending him to you when I meet with a good opportunity, as I suppose poor Nip is nearly done up by this time. Bran is very good natured and very courageous, no dog being able to cope with him in the two Provinces. He is about 2 years old, a native of Long-Island U.S., his Breed no one knows.

I have been rather unfortunate in family matters, Mrs. King having miscarried four times within 7 months after our marriage and I have now no appearance of being a papa.

I am afraid I am out of Mrs. Garricks good books at not having taken her advice, which was not to marry a widow, but was Mrs. Garrick to see her she would make an exception, and I hope, if Mrs. King makes her appearance in England both Mrs. G. and yourselves will honor her with your notice. Nature has been very bountiful to her in person, and mind and disposition, her education very limited. I am sure she would be a great favourite with you.

Hoping that Mrs. and Miss Rackett are well to whom I beg to be affectionately remembered

I remain, My dear friend
Your ever obliged and Grateful
Thomas King.

D-RAC/E/111. Part of a letter from Thomas King to Thomas Rackett.

No date. [The first page of the letter is missing]
Sir George Prevost[87] with about 23,000 Regulars, twenty thousand Militia well disposed, and a large body of hardy (?) Kreulich Indians is suffering seven or eight thousand vagabond Yankies to lay waste the country that they appear in! We are obliged to hide

86 Robert Fulton's *Clermont*, a steam paddle boat built in 1802, was the first known commercial steam boat in America. The success of this prompted other operators to begin coastal services. In 1817 a consortium started running services from Sacket's Harbor on Lake Ontario. The service mentioned by King may have developed from this venture.
87 Sir George Prévost (1767-1816), British General who was Commander in Chief in British North America (now Canada) during the war between Britain and the United States in 1812.

our diminished heads upon the Lakes! And with our Navy so far as I can observe there appears to be neither Zeal, skill or Enterprise except among the Merchant vessels of the Enemy. I do not feel very sorry at Brother Jonathan[88] taking a little of the shine out of them as it may tend to bend their disgusting haughtiness. Rogers is again out, if he falls in with any of our single frigates woe to them. We should have been in a pretty pickle in this part of the world had European affairs not taken so favourable a turn.

Our Surgeon joined the Regiment a few days ago and brought with him his wife who is a niece of your late friend Paul Senby.[89] There is a person in this town who has fifteen or twenty of his Paintings in water colour taken from Scenes in Italy &c.

I cannot for the life of me distinguish between what are called Drawings and Paintings. It appears to me that drawing may be applied to all kinds of shapes and figures on canvas, paper or any other substance. You must excuse my bad writing, bad language, Etc. Etc. as when I have a wish or thought to communicate, fearful of it slipping through my fingers, that I cannot attend to either. This apology must also serve for digressions and want of connection. My mind is bent more on things than on words. I wish I had our easy familiar language to unfold the production of nature and experience. I would then try and add to the entertainment of your fireside. The appreciation of ideas reminds me of the most rational part of my life spent there. How completely I have you pictured in my mind after the removal of the Table cloth. Mrs. R. on one side, you on the other, breaking out now and then, as though I am from a cloud, and Miss Dorothea on the left of her Mama, with a News-paper for a screen, saying, Papa – Papa – now you don't hear – Yes I do my dear – laying stress on the word do, and then rubbing the nasal process a little, to awaken and brighten the fancy aided by a Glass of good substantial Port! Whenever I think of comfort away I run to your fire-side, placing myself opposite to my friend Mrs. Rackett and on your Right with my wine Glass on the mantle-piece or just behind my right shoulder, on the side-board. Then for the amusing and instructive conversation, or well selected reading, each relieving the other. How happily you steer your Bark between levity &c. on the one hand and austerity &c. &c. on the other. In fact your skill in navigation is such that neither of those unsightly views are ever in sight, and a passenger was he only to travel in your Vessel, would not know, or he would gradually forget the fate which commonly attends others. What with designing and ignorant navigators (to keep up the Metaphor) it is with much observation and difficulty I can prevent them running down my bark, being obliged to work her with little or no help (putting aside my instructions before I departed), but as God rules this Physical world as well as the Moral I hope to get to my destined port without a great deal of damage, that there will be enough to keep me from sinking!

88 Brother Jonathan preceeded Uncle Sam as the personification of the United States. The sobriquet is thought to have been derived from Jonathan Turnbull, a friend of George Washington. (HSLD)

89 Paul Sanby R.A. (1731-1809) was an English map-maker turned watercolourist who mainly painted landscapes, extolled by Gainsborough as 'no better artist of real Views from Nature'. With his brother Thomas he was one of the founders of the Royal Academy in 1768. In his youth,Thomas Rackett studied drawing with the Sandby brothers.

Since writing the above an opportunity has offered for sending it, by a Merchant Ship for Grenock. I shall saddle our friend Knowles with the postage! I hope this will meet you settled in London for the winter, ours as yet, has been very moderate. We have had a great deal of controversy here about Lancaster's system of education [90]and Bible Societies lately introduced into this Province but it requires deep investigation before its utility can be decided upon. The most conspicuous figure on the lists is Dr. Croke Judge of the Admiralty and he is opposed to it. On the other hand the system is supported by the Governor Sir McSherbrooke[91] & most of the leading men, aided by almost the whole of the population, who are nearly all dissenters. Its unnecessary to wish you a pleasant Christmas, why should you not be as happy on that day as on any other? The cheerfulness that invariably prevails in your family circle, make your life a perpetual Jubilee.

I hope to have the remembrance of my dear friend Mrs. Rackett, Miss Dorothea, Dr. Maton, Dr. Tattersall, and Mr. & Mrs. Wray, not forgetting my factious friend Mrs. Garrick whose name you will read after Miss Dorothea's. I am delighted in thinking that some parts of this letter will not fail to please you, believe me, my dear and ever valued friend. If I was the cause either intentionally or innocently of giving you one moment's uneasiness it would embitter every moment of my existence. The more I see of the world, the more, I know how to appreciate your goodness to a wretched and helpless orphan.

Your affectionate
Thomas King.

D-RAC/E/104. Letter from Mrs. E. Pulteney to Miss Dorothea Rackett.

Lymington March 19, 1818
Having heard nothing of our Spettisbury Friends for a long time, except by mere chance, that they have not yet made their annual emigration, I take the advantage of a parcel going to Charles, to jog their memories on the subject of a long wished & expected letter; which is now the more desirable as the late tremendous weather renders it doubtful whether our distant Friends are living with a house over their heads; ours has been partly blown down, though without any serious injury to its inhabitants. but as I have just given Mrs. Farquharson an account of the disasters they have occurred in this vicinity, & as I do not like to tell a melancholy tale, twice if wish to hear it, I refer you to her. The Lizzard indeed, I think you will like to see, & if you are inclined to make the purchase, I believe it may yet be procured, though at a high price; & fortunate should we esteem ourselves if it should prove a sufficient encitement to bring you hither. You might easily make Lymington in your way to

90 Joseph Lancaster developed a system of education using the older pupils as monitors. It was popular in rural schools and overseas, as it enabled them to expand capacity without requiring extra teaching staff.

91 Sir John Coape Sherbrooke (1764-1830) was appointed Lieutenant-Governor of Nova Scotia in 1811.

London. for why should you always go dog-trotting the old way?

As a further temptation to Mr. Rackett, I inform him that Mr. Charles received yesterday a specimen of antique carving on which, if they were to lay their heads together, I know not what they might make of it. Will it have any sensible effect on Dorothea if I just whisper that we have two very handsome young Gentlemen at the next door, who will not continue much longer in their present abode? "Strike while the iron is hot". Further, to tempt the whole Trio, I add that last night I received from Leicestershire a budget of delightful charades, riddles &c. &c. If all this does not move you, I shall think you have al lost your energies, & that Dorothea in particular is fallen fast asleep. I wish she would awake, & become as fond of letter writing as Miss Seward[92]. Of her six thick volumes I have gone through one & a half, & though I should be more pleased if she did not evince so high an opinion of her own talents, great as I acknowledge them, I am really much entertained with them, & you would all be interested in what she says of your intimate acquaintances, Mrs Thrale-Piozzi, Dr Johnson, Mrs. Knowles (is the Mr. Knowles I have met at your house her son?), Mr. Nicholls & a thousand more. Nothing I think gives so intimate a knowledge of character as familiar letters, & her correspondents are mostly of the first class. Tho' we do not see many of their letters, we gather their sentiments from hers .... I have read as you Dorothea ordered me *Tales of my Landlord* but pardon me if I say I am somewhat disappointed; I quarrel with the title of one tale, *Old Mortality*[93] is by no means an interesting character, & has nothing to do with the story. Then the Misanthrope hero is too ugly & disgusting for a hero, his mode of life too impossible, beyond probable & his Character inconsistent. Can you tell me if Walter Scott is really the author?

But my prime favorite Dr. Franklin! I command you to read his *Memoirs*[94], If you wish to see the full extent of human powers, read him. How virtuous! How wise! How noble! How transcendant? There is one thing however, I lament to find towards the end of his life, the bitterness with which he speaks of the King. Whatever was wrong in his conduct ought to be imputed to the delusion which is usually practiced on Kings, for I believe his heart is pure. Dr. Franklin with his wonted candour should have thought this: 'tis true he lived among the Kings enemies, but this also he should have remembered.

Among the disasters of the storm, I forgot to tell Mrs. Farquharson of the fat old woman at the toll-bridge, who being unable to walk, when the water was knee-deep in the house, her son took her up to carry to her to a neighbour's house, but being unable was obliged to set her down in the water to get assistance. They had six pigs in the house, which in the darkness they could not attempt to rescue, but in the morning, great was their suprize, on finding them all alive, & floating on the water.

When you see our Stickland Friends, pray tell them with my kind regards, that I consider them as a letter in my debt.

92 Anna Seward (1742-1809) *Louisa, a Poetical Novel in Four Epistles*, 1784.

93 Sir Walter Scott's novel *Old Mortality* was published in 1816.

94 The *Memoirs* of Benjamin Franklin (1706-1790) were not published in his lifetime. Apart from French translations, the first three parts were first published together in English by Franklin's grandson, William Temple Franklin, in London in 1818.

I shall be glad to learn that Mrs. Blunt has quite recovered her health.

Accept the Love & kind wishes of all around me. I think it would do you good to see our children. The little Henry Frederick is a sweet plaything.
Adieu! E. Pulteney.

D-RAC/E/107. John Knowles of the Navy Office to Rev. T. Rackett.

Revd. Dear Sir,
I have for some time felt that I have treated you with neglect, and I have experienced all that wavering of mind which proceeds from a duty long delayed and the irresolution to repair, what you consider to be a fault. I trust however for forgiveness partly on this score, but more particularly from having been much engaged during the absence of Mr. Sippings in affording instruction to three Dutch gentlemen whom their government wish and ours have allowed to be instructed in the new principle of ship building.

I find them to be men of enlarged views, possessing science and knowledge of several languages, their english is so good that I have seldom occasion to call in the aid of a word of french. The government of a country are supposed to know but, but although I am a friend to liberality, I doubt the policy of allowing foreigners to profit by all the expence, labour and experience which have been called into action during the last 14 years to bring this system to its present perfection. I am sorry to say that I have had a distressing letter from the Countess de Barde, she has lost the hope of her family, the eldest son, he died at the age of eleven years; I not only feel for that amiable woman his mother, but I really have regret for one to whom I was much attracted, having lived in the same house with him at that period when a child engages itself to you by its harmless and amusing prattle. As yet I have not written to the Countess and I hardly know whether to do it now; or to delay it for a time; sometimes consolation comes too soon and often too late by opening an healing wound. In a fortnight I accompany Mr. Fuseli to the sea coast, I look for much pleasure from the excursion; I am sure of instruction. Mr. Beltz[95] has paid me a visit, I do wish to cultivate his acquaintance he appears to be an amiable man with a cultivated mind.

You have no doubt seen the *exposée* of Drury Lane Theatre. I fear the burthen is too heavy to bear; this is far from being serviceable to the other house for it depreciates theatrical property. I have called several times at your dwelling and have always had a favourable report, no complaint of any kind, the house appears to be clean and in good order. I am sorry that I have nothing to communicate which will amuse you. my life (at this season in London) is somewhat like that of a horse in a mill, to and from Somerset house make up the sum of my peregrinations, and while there employed in business less capable of instruction than amusement what then can you expect from dullness, thus rendered more dull?

Captain Raggett is to be appointed to generalship, I have this day written to

95 George Beltz was co-executor to Mrs. Garrick, with the Rev. Thomas Rackett. (HSLD)

him in favour of Mr. Brice and I hope it will succeed. Portsmouth or Plymouth would really be a comfortable station for him, as these good things are much sought after, I fear I shall not be successful, if so, he must take the will for the deed. My kindest respects and regards are due to your family, I hope Mrs. Rackett has been free from her complaint and that your daughter enjoys her usual good health and spirits. I fear I have already tired you with many words about nothing, but be assured that no one subscribes himself with more truth – Your affectionate friend and devoted servant than

John Knowles,
Navy Office, 15th Augt. 1818.

D-RAC/D/78. Letter from Mrs. Maria Blunt[96] to Mrs. T. Rackett.

Enham House, June 25th 1823.
I have a great longing my dear Friend for one of your nice letters. How are you all, the better for being amused – and the better amused, while you have those you love to partake of your enjoyments. We who have lost the cheerful society of our home circle for six weeks and who have been chilling and starving upon our cogitations, know well what your feelings are. If you have escaped the notice of the dangerous Monster in London, the Influenza – you may be thankful, as I am, that amidst the severe attacks of fever, colds and rheumatism raging universally, and among all ages and ranks, I get only a nipping now and then in my bones, - and a few gentle touches, to remind me that the wind is in the east, which is neither good for Woman nor Beast.

Harriet thank God, has taken herself in hand as a Patient and very successfully, with the aid of the Acid Bath (heretofore so beneficially taken) or we had been sojourners at this time at Cheltenham. Our family went by steam-packet[97] June 4th to Scotland – My son convoyed them thither, paid his duty to his Father & Mother-in-law for a fortnight; and will I trust return to Enham this week.

You see in the papers how celebrated our County is become of late in its exhibitions of Roman Antiquities? –

Within a few miles of this spot the pavement of a great Roman General's Tent[98], as supposed to be, was discovered about 2 feet under the surface, by the farmer's Servants while ploughing, & the Villa; which (it) describes as of celebrity, is on Mrs. Greenwood's estate at Brookwood[99], Near Alresford Hants not more than a mile out

96 Anna Maria Blunt (1748-1829) daughter of Sir Thomas Gatehouse. Enham House was where Jane Austen had attended her first ball in October 1792.

97 In 1801 William Simmington built the *Charlotte Dundas* paddle boat, powered by a Boulton and Watt steam engine, which worked on the Forth and Clyde canal. Henry Bell's *Comet* of 1812, also working on the Clyde, started a rapid expansion of steam boat services.

98 Mrs. Blunt seems to have known that Julius Caesar had a portable mosaic mounted in a frame carried with him on his campaigns, as stated by Suetonius, *Divus Iulius*, 46. (HSLD)

99 This discovery is recorded in *Sketches of Hampshire, Embracing the Architectural Antiquities, Topography, etc.* by John Duthy, 1839.

of the high road from Farnham to Winchester. Whether it had been handed down to them by tradition or by inspiration that large treasures were underground in store for them, I cannot learn – but that the Relatives of the family have been of late indefatigable in their pursuit, we may credit from the result – These will be amusing testing places for the antiquarians, in their tour to Fonthill Abbey, which is now in the full display of beauties of nature and art in great magnificence. I am picturing to my eye the forest of American and other exotic Plants, which report says are thriving as if they were in their native soil. Ours here, which are of humbler growth, have shewn off, and deserved notice this year. The rains suit them. If Edwd. had a place of his own I should be for beautifying his Gardens. What are the Daveys the Nurserymen doing? Selling cuttings of curious Geraniums, at so much a bundle? Is it true that Mrs. Davey has made £400 by a new Geranium which they call Daviania? Is it what I hear of a dark crimson colour and a large flower?

I am not very much addicted to the forms of etiquette or before this I ought to have congratulated you upon Mr. H. Davis's marriage which I do with as much satisfaction as if I had written a week ago for that sole purpose. His dear Mother is now in part to be comforted for past sorrows I wish them all the happiness they can enjoy together, pray tell Lady Davis this, with our congratulatory regards.

Perhaps in your way homewards you will peep in upon us? Our beds are always well-aired; and it would give us sincere pleasure to have a little chat with Mr. R. & yourself once more.

We have read "*Quentin Durward*" though it is of a different character to the earlier Novels, attributed to Sir Walter Scott, in our opinion, this is equal if not superior to them in interest and excellence. I can say for myself that it did not give me the pause of a minute for anxious expectation, or fearful interested fermentations; so strong has he marked his persons and their deeds – You will remember we read it aloud – and are living in the Country quiet, - secluded from those interruptions unavoidable in great Towns and which naturally divide attention. – Let me know how you are all going on soon, Harriet desires to be as kindly remembered by all, and to you all as does your ever faithful friend
A.M.B.

Will you be kind enough if you can to get some who are Subscribers to the "School for the Indigent Blind", (Lady Davis and many of the Solly family are down in the list) to give their votes for the poor Boy whose case I inclose, & if you will be good enough to remind your friend Mr. Beltz of Poor Sarah Burridge I will thank you much. As my Harriet made me a nice pen – I am ashamed of the number of blots in my letter. Where are the Sollys?[100] I hope well and happy?

100 Dorothea, daughter of Thomas Rackett married Samuel Solly at St Paul's, Covent Garden on 26 January 1821.

D-RAC/D/ 81. Letter from Thomas Rackett to Mrs. Rackett.

February 1825.
My dr. Love,
I write a few lines as I suppose you will like to hear how I am getting on. I am still very busy, putting the prints to rights as they have been so much disturbed by being taken to the Masters office, and I cannot put off having them in proper order. I have not yet had time to see anyone, not even Dr. Maton as my mornings have been all occupied. I stated to the Master the manner in which the Mulberry boxes were ordered by Mrs. Carr[101] and Mr. Deane as they wanted to make us account for the Mulberry wood and pay for it. But they are to be left entirely out of the Masters report, and as they are in Mr. Deans hands we can have any we choose paying for the workmanship. The large dressing cases and work boxes which I believe come to about 30s. if I recollect what Mr. Tane told me last year. The small boxes of course are much less but I don't know exactly what they will be. I am going to find out (from) Mr. Tane who made them if I can to day. The Mulberry tree[102] that remains will of course be sold and I suppose will fetch a good price, but you know we have a piece of our own.

I saw Mr Beltz yesterday who enquired much after you. I was at the R. Society on Thursday which was very well attended but did not see anybody particular but Mr. Nichols and Mr. Caley.

Mr. Penn the Governor of Portland[103] is about to have some mark of His Majesty's approbation conferred upon him and Mr. Beltz is to see him this morning respecting his Coat of Arms. He is to take the Arms of Penn but is to have an augmentation. He has chosen a Wapety[104] but he must have something on the upper part of the field. Mr. Beltz desired me to suggest something to him that might be produce of Pennsylvania. I recommended two ears of Zea Mays or Indian corn. His supporters to be two Indians so that Indian corn is very appropriate. I also recommended that one of the Indians should have the belt of wampum in his hand. The other is to have the treaty made by his ancestor with the Indians in his hand.

I sent you the papers with the debates on the Catholic Association bill[105]. I shall know more in a few days about the business I am come about but now take this to Mr. Knowles who quits at two o'clock. I hope the travellers returned safe from Salisbury. I dined with Mr. Knowles one day.
I remain, Yours affectionately, T.R.

101 Wife of Mrs. Garrick's solicitor. (HSLD)

102 The Mulberry tree appears to be the remains of the pieces of the famous tree (at New Place, bought by Shakespeare) cut down in 1756 by The Rev. Francis Gastrell, and bought by Garrick, and Tomas Sharpe of Stratford. (HSLD)

103 John Penn (1760-1834), grandson of William, founder of Pennsylvania, was appointed Governor of Portland by George III and built Pennsylvania Castle (in reality a country house) for himself on Portland between 1797 and 1800.

104 This is the American Wapitsi. (HSLD)

105 Sir Francis Burdett proposed a Catholic Emancipation Bill in 1825, one of a series to be put forward during this period. The proposal to allow Roman Catholics to worship openly was politically divisive and it was not until 1829 that the Catholic Emancipation Act was passed.

D-RAC/D/78. Letter from Mrs. M. Blunt to Mrs. T. Rackett.

Enham House
20th Sept. (1825)
My dear Friend,
As the removal of celebrated personages is generally announced in the papers, where I have sought in vain to find yours:- in friendship, you, or one of your fraternity, might I think, have strained a muscle for once in a way, just to say where you are – and that you were in tolerable health. You know how I wish you to be so. I will hope that you have joined in the Chorus with the gay ones – that you enjoyed the Blandford Races, and are amending in every way since your return to Spetisbury. Mr. Rackett too, if he takes to riding on horse back, will become a new Man. Exercise is an excellent means of health, if moderate, and regular; but those who extend it to labour and toil; must sooner, or later, find out their mistake.

The Sollys are with you I daresay – I wish you were all within visiting distance of us? Mrs. Edward Blunt averse to quitting home till the latest moment went to Kensington on Monday ye. 5th and on Wednesday, viz. ye. 7th, at 3 in the morning was safely delivered of a fine Boy; she continues remarkably well, and this time is early become a good nurse; and No. 6 plays his part admirably in this new world, tis happy when these events succeed well, and go on smoothly. Mrs. Fenwick, Judge Burroughs[106] Daughter, is as active as ever in her productions – she treated with a fourth on the same day. I am happy to say my Friends of Abbotts Anne are looking more like well, than I have of late beheld them. Miss Burrough the Niece they say is somewhat relieved by the Sea-air. They are now at Laverstoke and the Laver into the bargain. The Chief Justice and his Lady are expected there. We are enjoying ourselves as much as we can do in Shirley's absence; Miss Forbes & Emily are our inmates, they suit well in their tastes and habits. The Sawbridges have been here for a few days, and brought their niece a Barwell with them a nice Girl of 7 yrs. & ½ old, who was consigned to her care by her brother in India, at 4 years old; when she appeared like a Hottentot in all her native wildness – is now entirely by her Aunt's teaching a well improved Girl. I like that our young wild-shoots should be trained & train themselves upon such models. It is astonishing how much more quickly example teaches, from the young – than all our musty lessons.

The Harris's being at Doles Lodge[107] is a most comfortable circumstance to us. He has taken it till December for the remainder of Mrs. Lloyd's term. They seem to like it, and I see already the good effects of the air, and interesting employment on Mrs. Harris's health. Edward having a turn for mechanics has had a steam-bath made

106 Probably Sir James Burrough (1749-1837). Appointed Justice of the Court of Common Pleas, he was knighted in 1816.

107 Doles Lodge, built of chalk block, stood near the site of the present house at Doles, and was pulled down about the time the new house was built by the Dewar family in the early 1860s. At the time when Mrs. Blunt was writing both Enham House and Doles Lodge were being rented, the former by herself, the latter by Mrs. Lloyd who was sub-letting it to Mr. & Mrs. Harris. D.A.B. Dewar, the owner of both properties was living in London, and was the great-grandfather of H.S.L. Dewar, Editor of the Thomas Rackett papers. (HSLD)

– and by a Country Operator which turns out well – we have coaxed her twice to use it & I have great hopes that already some benefit has been derived from it – in abating the constant state of inflamation she endures, & a burning skin. They have had some very choice visitors with them, Sr. Geo. & Lady Scovell & Miss Bradshaw her niece who were too agreeable, not to leave a blank behind when they took themselves off.

Where is Lady Davis? I hear Mrs. Greathead is coming to pay her mother a visit in England. Mr. & Mrs. G., I am told have been at Vienna. The Brickdales are living near them and like them much. Mrs. B. I am sure they will find an acquisition. Now tell me if you are going on feeding yourself by little and little as you so laudably began to do? And tell me whether you are pursuing other remedies required by the Learned in the Medical line. Tell me how reading goes on – how music prospers – what books have fallen under your notice, and how your Garden grows. Our apples are remarkably fine and abundant this year. Our Pear-trees are bearing for the first year – the Alves's were they to come again to this place would reap many advantages from the great expence they were at in their Garden. They are to come in October to Lady Dallas at Brighton – but we hear are to go back again to Italy – I wish Edwd. had either a place he could call his own, or the promise of a firm footing at Enham for 20 years to come. He has lived long enough here to have grown fond of the place and I should be sorry if he must turn out.

We are reading *Bonaparte's Expedition to Russia* by Segur[108] who has contrived to make the book interesting by his animated descriptions of the true likeness he paints of his Master Napoleon. Madame de Genlis' *Memoires*[109] are worth reading, tho' 6 volumes. Shirley trotted and gallop'd thro' dozens of Books during our absence the names are now not at hand. This scrawl will be no inducement I fear to give me an answer? I have scribbled away without sense or reason.

Edwd. has built a dwarf double Phaeton a very nice & elegant Carriage with 4 wheels I have had several drives in it & in Mrs. Harris's more Gigantic open Barouche & I have visited many of the neighbours – There's for you! A joint letter let me have soon – Harriet and Emily join in kind remembrance to your party with My dear Mrs. R.
Your very affectionate
M. Blunt
Ed. is at Wallop to meet Geo. Harris & to shoot.

D-RAC/D/81. Letter from Th. Rackett to Mrs. Rackett. No date, but written after the death of Mrs. Garrick in 1822, perhaps 1825.

My dear Love,
I write a few lines to day as I suppose you will like to hear how I am going on. I have

108 *History of the Expedition to Russia*, by General Count Phillipe de Ségur, published 1825.
109 *Mémoires inédits sur le XVIII' siècle* by Caroline Félicite Stéphanie, Madame de Genlis, published 1825.

been very busy ever since I came to Town. I was at the Master's Office yesterday for 4 hours & I had to carry a large box of prints in a coach for inspection. The Proceedings before the Master have gone on to my entire satisfaction, he has put the opposite side upon giving proof of all or most of the things they claim, as having belonged to Mr. Garrick. We are not therefore obliged to shew of evidence or give proof of what belongs to her except in a very few instances. We had all the curiosities, Rings, Mulberry Cup Etc. to shew before the Master yesterday. The latter article is not yet decided on. We go on again on Tuesday. I am in great hopes that the snuff boxes will be permitted to go to the Nephews as the Family see to give out they will not oppose their having them if they are adjudged to belong to the next of kin. The enquiry is conducted with .... liberality. Many of the valuables will come to the Executors for the benefit of Madam de Saay. I have had a letter from her, which when Mr. Beltz has seen I will send you if I can.

I have not been able to get a paper containing an account of Davis versus the Bank of England[110] nor have I had time to transcribe it, but I have read it and it is very strongly in favour of H.D. All the Judges are decidedly in his favour and make some very pointed observations. If you have not seen it, I will try to get one, but it is long to write.

I dined yesterday with D. Maton, Mrs. & Miss Wray, & Mrs. Charles Maton & R. Pilkington. Mr. Wray could not be there. Dr. Maton recommends you to take a little Castor Oil for your giddiness, but not too much, and I hope there is now no occasion for any. I was in hopes to hear how you were to day but I do not wish you to write when it is troublesome. Mr. Beltz, Dr. M. and all the rest of the party desire to be kindly remembered to you. I saw Mr. Brande at the R. Society on Thursday, Hatchett is better and is at Brighton where he means to stay till next Xmas. I also saw Mr. Caley, who enquired much after you. I dined with Mr. Knowles on Tuesday, he shewed me his beautiful Snuff box from the Late King of France. It is most elegant and the workmanship very fine, the Letter L in diamonds beneath a crown of diamonds. The Ring from the King of Sweden has his initials C.J. Charles John in a Circle of diamonds, and is a very elegant and valuable present. I am to dine with him on Tuesday to meet the Swedish Ambassador, Baron Seguier the French Minister .... Chancellor of France, etc.

The Masters curiosity was so much excited by some of the prints that he requested to look them over and I have left them with him, the Key of the box to examine them at his leisure. Dr. Maton was obliged to go out according to his usual practice in the afternoon and did not return before 10 when we all departed. I have not yet seen Miss Davies the weather being very bad and dirty. I have now I think told you all I know & must take this to Mr. Knowles as he leaves his office at two o'clock and it is now past one. With love to Lady Davis, I remain,

Yours affectionately

T.R.

110 *The case of Davis v. Bank of England* was heard in 1824, further helping to date this letter. The case related to the Bank's permitting a transfer of company stock under a forged power of attorney, and continues to be quoted in the 21st century as a landmark case in the law of restitution.

D-RAC/D/81. P.S. Letter from Thos. Rackett to Mrs Rackett.

Wed. Feb. 1st 1826.
There was it seems a great squabble between Brande[111] and Sir H. Davey at a Meeting of the Managers of the Royal Institute. Brande accused Sir H. of converting one of his discoveries to his own benefit, and sir H. being in the Chair moved that B. should leave the room and on a division, having committed his motion to writing, he had only three hands in favour of it, but I apprehend I shall hear a great deal more, and farther particulars anon. One thing is certain, that the disputes and squabbles of Philosophers prove of no advantage to Science! Happily there are no philosophic Lawyers, so that they must settle their differences in their own way by themselves. This affair one may suppose has made a good deal of noise. Mr. Daniel (not T.F.D.) espoused the cause of Mr. B. and observed that it would be as proper for Sir H.D. to leave the room himself.

D-RAC/D/78. Letter from Mrs. M. Blunt to Mrs. Rackett.

Enham House, Nov. 11th 1826
My dear Friend
When opportunities present themselves for doing what we wish, and ought to do, tis a pity, in a fluctuating scene like ours on earth, not to catch the moment as it flies. .... Your letter I hope was written at intervals, and only when ease & convenience dictated? if so I shall have more pleasure, in receiving others from you. You please me by telling me that you attend to your diet &c. as we advance in years we are compelled to do it. & as the strength of our organization decreases, we are bound in reason, to abate its labours; if we do not, the result falls miserably upon ourselves; and who would not avoid pain if possible to do so? I am glad to hear you are stronger than you were, daily drives out, will make you more so – and keep up your spirits. After taking a blue O, I am for your trying Huxham's Tincture[112] – of bark, beginning with a good tea-spoonful every day an hour before dinner – I have adopted this plan with success.

I hope our friend Mr. Rackett continues active in the country, as well as in Town? Tho' objects are far more distant from his research, and not many of them so attractive to a mind like his; during Mr. Solly's absence, he must, being his own Purveyor, exert himself more than usual, or agreeable, in pursuit of them.

Harriet has had a nice long letter from Dorothea who writes cheerfully though by the invalidism of their stud their equestrian feats are for a time at a stand. Their Piano too is not in musical harmony with their feelings & the Tuner whoever he be who having looked after two different journies, at it, was so fastidious, as to refuse the Office of mending it.

111 William Thomas Brande (1788-1866) F.R.S. (HSLD) Succeeded Sir Humphry Davy in the chair of Chemistry at the Royal Institution. He married Anna the daughter of Charles Hatchett.

112 Huxham's tincture of bark, devised by Dr. John Huxham (1692-1768).

It would be delightful to procure the receipt for setting or more properly, fixing Chalk & pencil drawings – Emily Shirley & Miss Smith, who draws well, are all busy in the art when they lay their heads together - & it does not suit my old Maidish love of cleanliness, to have the slopping of milk over tables and carpets.

The good Burroughs I have not seen for 6 weeks – I go out but little, except in the Greenhouse, & in the Sunshine – by the side of our house – I dare not venture into cold or moist draughts of air. I live all the Morning in my own room – dine, except in very large parties, and spend the evening down stairs. My dear Harriet amuses herself a good deal in the Garden and Greenhouse, and is remarkably well, without entering deeply into the scientific part of botany – the culture of Shrubs and flowers may be an amusing pursuit. When we talk with many of our learned neighbours, the Kerrs for instance we lower our towering crests. – so do our plants, when they are by.

We are reading the memoirs of Reynolds the Dramatist[113] they are very entertaining; so we thought Kemble's & I dare say we shall find Mrs. Siddon's. – it seems an odd plan the giving us a biography of a living subject. I can hardly suppose, but that much truth is suppressed, and the facts published in favour; not to be highly coloured. *Brambletye House* we like, & *Tor Hill*[114], a quite new Historical novel, we are prepared to approve. I am reading a very cheerfully-written little Vol. of a *6 Months Tour in the West Indies* by A. Coleridge[115]; nephew of the Bishop. You will give us hints in this way whenever you write

You know our friend Miss Butts is married – the young man has an amiable physiognomy, and is gentlemanly. And she will have plenty of money – so I hope they will be happy.

I delight in the thought of our dear Lady Davis being so near you, and coming to spend some time with you. I have just commenced a bettering nutritious plan of Lady Imhoffs for her old Aunt Barebones; which is to boil sheeps' trotters, well cleaned, to a jelly, which during the boiling is to be often scummed; put a tea-cup full of milk (in which boil Cinnamon, lemon peel & Sugar) to the same quantity of the Jelly when strained through a sieve. This, try my good friend – Lady D. I know will second my proposal. With many kind regards to you and your better Half from me and all mine here, I will make a *finis* – and assure you that I am,

Ever warmly yrs.

M.B.

113 Frederic Reynolds (1764-1841) wrote nearly a hundred lightweight comedies and tragedies which attracted temporary popularity. In 1826 he published his memoir, *The Life and Times of Frederic Reynolds.*

114 *Brambletye House* and *Tor Hill,* both published in 1826, novels by Horace Smith (1779-1849) a member of Shelley's circle, who took part with him in a sonnet-writing competition.

115 *Six Months in the West Indies in 1825* was published anonymously in 1826. Its author was Henry Nelson Coleridge, nephew of the Bishop of Barbados.

D-RAC/D/81. Thomas Rackett to Mrs. Rackett. Jan. 11. 1827.

I went out early yesterday morning, to Mr. Beltz on business, and being requested to dine with him *en famile,* did not return till evening & found your letter, by which I am very glad to find you are better and that you had a pleasant day on Monday. I am very well and take very good care of myself & a few friends take very good care of me, they will not let me be by myself at dinner, but I have enough to do in the morning, at home and abroad.

I sent to the Sollys a Fish and a few *bons bons* in a basket for their party & one to Horace Davis that they might all feast on Monday. I had yesterday a letter from Dorothea and Mr. Solly to acknowledge the receipt of it & that it came in very opportunely. They had their tenants children to choose King & Queen, & who were highly delighted. She has written for some mourning things in her room which I must look out to send her.

I dined on Sunday by invitation at the Wrays, with Dr. Maton, and they all enquired much after you and are all very well, & on Monday I dined at Dr. Maton's. Mr. Wray also dined here, no one else, and we had a great deal of chat about his tour, & cordial reception by the Landgravine of Hesse Homberg, and the Duke of Cambridge at Hannover, with a description of the City of Hesse Homberg, Hannover, Palace of Herenhausen &c. with various adventures, which befell him and Lord Talbot. They were both greatly pleased at their excursion.

At Vienna they were overturned in the Ambassadors carriage at Schoenbrunn, and as Lady E. Wellesley like <u>some other foolish people</u> would not get in again were forced to walk four miles to Vienna. The paper in the Gentleman's Magazine from Sir R.H. is in the Mag. for December published the 1st of January, which if Simmonds had not sent you must enquire for it. There is likewise in the Magazine a biographical Memoir of the late Mrs. Nicholls, with the portrait. Mr. Nicholls whom I have seen has sent me a copy of it with a fine impression of her portrait. You need not send me the Salisbury paper as all the papers are filled with Mr. D. of York, nor to the Sollys, I sent them a paper, so that I think you need not send any this week, though what I sent was not the Englishman.

We had some snow one night, but Sunday it thawed and disappeared. I should have liked to have partaken of your good fire and merriment on Monday, but we have a fine Turkey at Mr. Wrays, and a boiled leg of Pork at Dr. Matons so that I am not starved, though I am very economical when left to myself.

I called on Mr. Palmer a day or two ago & he assured me that he had received the Draught safely but that he did not acknowledge it, as he did not know where to direct his letter, Lady D. not having mentioned where she was staying. He has no doubt but that J.H.D. has received the books long 'ere this as they were regularly consigned by the usual agent and he was sent the Invoice to Horace Davis who will of course write particulars to J.H.D. He says they must be too precipitate in Mrs. Scotts affair but the money is lodged in Chancery & he hopes H. Davis will be able to get possession of it with her concurrence when the matter is represented to her in the proper light. I send you an Enigma which was put into my hands by the Author.

ENIGMA
My voice is the sweetest that ever was heard
I my feelings express without saying a word,
The Warrior abash, and the Coward make bold
The worthless and faithless wherever I'm sold
Yet if given or won, so high is my worth,
There is nothing so valued, so dear upon Earth.
Jew, Christian and Turk, at my shrine bend the knee
Een Atheists become true believers for me,
Tho' by Heaven ordain'd and in Holy writ seen,
Neglected, forbidden, condemned I have been.
I'm lawfull, unlawfull, I'm wicked, I'm good,
By millions I'm made, yet by few understood,
I'm pleasing, I'm teasing, I'm young, I am old,
I make people do, what they never wish told.
The King and the Beggar I visit the same
So if you won't feel me – at least tell my Name.
W.G.F.

I am now under the necessity of going out and perhaps shall not return till I take this to Mr. Knowles, I have not been able to discover anything more respecting the Thieves nor has any attempt been made, I shall therefore I hope shortly return but I shall have business to occupy me for a few days. The Maid appears to be carefull and indeed fearful enough now. Least I should have time to say more I shall now conclude, with love to Lady Davis.
Yours affectly.
T.Rackett

D-RAC/D/81. Letter from Th. Rackett to Mrs. Rackett.

Jan. 16 – 1827
My dear Love,
I write a line to day for fear you whould be in hourly expectation of me, to say that I shall not be able to fix my return for 2 or 3 days in consequence of some curious circumstances, which I cannot fully detail in this Letter (I shall take care to look out the things you have mentioned.) A person having applied to Lord Radnor for a contribution, he has enclosed the letter to me, & I have this day written to his Lordship & must wait till I receive his answer. I write this at the Navy Office. You are mistaken respecting the Author of the Enigma, as you will perceive by the following lines which I sent to the author myself.

Omnia Vincit Amor
As I mus'd on my pillow deaf, drowsy, and stupid

I methought was address'd in these words by blind Cupid,
Wake and learn what you seek from the Sparrow & Dove,
What subdues all mankind, can be nothing but Love.

This produced a Poetic reply which I cannot now transcribe not having it in my pocket. However I have communicated the Poetic solution from Spettisbury to the true Author who appears much pleased and flattered therewith.

I have seen Mr. Miles[116], who has some prospect & great hopes of obtaining a situation at the Museum. Mr. Solly has likewise written in his favour to two of his friends there and Sir Richard has made the greatest exertions in his behalf. He, Mr. M. has also received one Hundred pounds of Royal Bounty so that he is in good plight and good spirits.

There being no meeting of the Learned Societies I accompanied Mr. Knowles on Saturday to Covent Garden Theatre to see the Pantomime of Mother Shipton in which there is an admirable Cat, very well performed, a great deal of fine Scenery, Rope dancing, a Baloon, &c. &c. I am to dine to day with Dr. M. who it appears is furnishing his House in the most expensive Manner. The furniture of the dining parlour & study having cost £500. The cabinet work is indeed very excellent and all new.

The book for Mrs. Munro is safe, but she has not called for it. Mr. Knowles desires his best respects to you and Lady Davis, & with my love to you both.
I remain, Yours affectly.
T.Rackett.

D-RAC/C/62. Rev. T. Rackett's draft letter to W. Pilkington, dt. Jan. 22, 1827.

My dear Sir,
Mr. Solly positively asserts that the Pamphlet was written at the invitation and for the benefit of Mr. Henry Pilkington who said he had been invited to supply the Quarterly Review with an article for the benefit of Agriculture. The 4ly Review however delayed inserting it because it did not coincide with his opinion. Mr. Solly recommended sending it to some other journal because it would not give the argument sufficient notoriety & sent an extract of a 2d letter from his friend connected with the 4ly Review offering to speak favourably of it if it was published. Mr. Solly therefore undertook to make the additions necessary to form it into a pamphlet if Mr. Pilkington would

116 W. A. Miles (1796-1851) believed himself the illegitimate son of William IV, baptised four and half years after his birth to a father whose names William Augustus Miles he adopted as his own. He conducted and published some competent excavations, but was obsessed with the idea of a Phoenician colony at Kimmeridge and the existence of a large altar of 'coal money' at Tyneham. He spent much time pestering the government or the Crown for funds or appointments. In 1829 he spent over 3 months in the Marshalsea debtor's prison. In 1840 the Speaker of the House of Commons recommended him as Superintendent of Police in Sydney, Australia, where, after frequent complaints he was forced to leave office at the end of 1849.

publish it. The success of the pamphlet depended entirely on its receiving notoriety through Mr. Pilkington's literary connections before mentioned. His friend did not exert himself so much as to secure it a reception in the shop of his own publisher Murray & no steps were taken to make it known except by Advertisement & bills posted at Doncaster.

Mr. Pilkington's invitation to Mr. S. to undertake the task originated in Mr. P's idea of the beneficent nature of the opinion contained in a pamphlet written by Mr. Solly, & of which he had presented a copy to Mr. Pilkington.

The expence of the publication was a trifle compared with Mr. Pilkington's interest in the subject. It was of great importance to him to shew that 40s per Qu: was not as Lord Milton had intended a fair and natural price for wheat in consequence of the Peace & the changes in the currency.

Mr. Solly hopes that the advice he gave Mr. Pilkington to keep his wheat has proved beneficial to him. When he first gave it wheat was selling at 40s. & during the following spring it rose to near 70s. Mr S. attributed the depression in the market to the discouragement of speculation by Government measures, and by erronious opinions and he prophesied that a depression from such causes must produce a reaction. Mr Pilkington afterwards acknowledged that he had prophesied truly.

However if Mr. Pilkington does not think himself sufficiently indemnified, Mr. Solly is willing to bear a part of the expence although he does not consider himself responsible for the failure of a publication when the conditions upon which it was undertaken have not been fulfilled.

Upon an impartial view of the subject I will venture to recommend that one of the parties should pay £15. and the other the remainder of the bill of £34.11. Upon receiving the whole of the work in Mr. Sheardown's possession. Mr. H. Pilkington having the option as to which share of the bill shall be discharged by him.

D-RAC/E/108. Letter from Lady Davis, sister of Mrs. T. Rackett to Mrs. Rackett.

Bath. March 15th 1827.
I begin my letter my Dearest Sister as you do that I may go on by degrees and have your last nice chatty one by me that I may begin with noticing what you have observed to me; much do I indeed wish that we were near enough together to communicate side by side ones thoughts and persuits, more particularly as writing is not one of the occupations that quite agree with you, especially when that detestable pain in the leg prevents a free motion of the arm; I have not had a return of it since I left off wine and my roasted Apples continue to agree with me so well that I have only once had recorse [sic] to magnesia for my benefit and when the weather changes, or I trust it will soon do, I hope by having more exercise I shall get strong and hearty; pray therefore follow my abstemious plan and refrain from eating anything that is greasy or fat firmented [sic] Liquors also and vegetables must not be indulged in and lastly I must urge you to be careful to taking cold.

You did not say whether you had kept both Tittoes or if one of them proves a male. I have not been able to get Almack's[117] but perhaps I shall be able to read it to better advantage if I can get a key to it as I hear there is one published for six pence. I am so interested in the perusal of the reign of George 3d – and there is so much else reading in it that I have sought for no other book, nor have I heard anybody speak of Head's *Rough Sketches*[118], so do not wait for me. I am quite glad to hear that the itching in your neck has ceased and I was delighted with Davis' letter, so my mind is at rest on that head; but I am rather fidgeted at not being able to hear of a person to be of comfort to you; Bath is overwelmed [sic] with gaiety altho' we have not only strict remonstrances from the Pulpit every Sunday Morning and a Lecture every Wednesday during Lent to condemn the practice of so much dissipation, this in part keeps all hands employ'd and renders it difficult at present to accomplish my wishes.

Sr. Walter James has taken a house at Cheltenham for six week, in the meantime his old Aunt Mrs. C. Holt has died and her Will has caused great surprise to many of the Family, it was supposed she would have died possessed of about five or six thousand pounds and had at times declared that most of it was to be Sr. Walters, but she burned that will a year before her end, leaving nearly thirty thousand pounds and bequeathing most of it to an Admiral Wilsons family of the same relationship as Sr. Walter and leaving the latter only one thousand pounds in the three Pr. Cents; this he has given in equal portions to his two Daughters Lady Bing and Mrs Davis the latter also comes in for a legacy of two hundred pounds. She has left upwards of seven Hundred pounds to her upper house Servant who had been faithful to her for many years and also a great part of her furnature [sic] china, glass &c. She was 94 years of age which I think rather too old to make a fresh will. There is another Lady in Bath that will be 100 years old in August, perhaps she may save her relations a similar (one word illegible Ed.) her name is Calvert. A relation of hers has sent me a card to a concert to hear the Messrs. Hermans, four Brothers who I am told by a great conoisure [sic] are the finest performers on different instruments that have been heard in this country for many years. I am now almost ashamed my Dearest Sister to look back upon the date of this, tho thank God it has not been delayed on account of bad health, the truth is that I have been much engaged and have myself given three dinners since my return to Bath, my object was the being as civil as I could to Mr. Robert Glyn and Mrs. Knipe of Epsom, the first on account of Lady Glyns constant attention to me and the latter for her own sake.

I gain'd great credit for the Elegance of my dinner last Tuesday, most of which I had from a very noted Cook and Confectioner in this place. I shall write it down to amuse you. "Soup, a beautiful Brill and Excellent Lobster Sauce which were removed for a small fillet of Veal and elegant little ham of 4pd. and quarter ornamented with cut flowers (from turnips and carrots). Corners Larded pullets with forcemeat and a fillet of chicken, Lobster patees and Croquetes. Second course; a larded Galina bottom, the finest seacale I ever saw, four corners orange jelly, Noyeau browne French

117 A well known Club and Assembly Rooms. The reference here seems to be so a circular issued by its committee of 12 ladies of rank in connection with the 12 week series of balls, etc. (HSLD)

118 Probably *Rough Notes*, by Sir Francis Head, Bart. (1793-1875), published in 1826. (HSLD)

pastries of various sweet meats, and an open Tart of magnum-bonum plums. They were all nicely and knowing whence they came I had no fidgets and therefore enjoyed my friends to the number of eight, we were very cheerful and Chatty and it went off extremely well; in the Evening I had invited a few just enough to make up a Loo table and one at Cassino.[119]

The next day I invited Florence (for Mrs. Davis does not go out as she still nurses her child) to go with me to see a very fine House that was on sale about five miles from Bath on the London Road, that is to say through Bath Easton, it is called Wesley House, it is built in the Gothic Style and is placed in a most beautiful Valley surrounded with high Hills, finely wooded and the River Avon meandering through the grounds; it has been purchased by a Mrs. Ricardo and must require a large Establishment both within and without. We were delighted with it and returned to a scrap dinner from the abundance of the day before, we were then both invited to hear these wonderful Germans play and sing, the one that performs on the Violincello is certainly very surprising but the German language and manner of singing I confess does not suit my taste so altho' these men are violently cried up I did not go to their concert this morning which they give [sic] at the public rooms at five shillings a Tickett.

The winds have been tremendous which has kept me from walking to the cottage but Mrs. Davis has the child brought to me and comes herself, I think she has very little milk but the Infant takes a great deal of food, so that I think it thrives tho it is certainly a very small child; but if you heard Horace talk of him, you would be led to imagine he was nearly a giant, the little thing has been Vaccinated twice, the first time it did not take, but I believe now it is going on well. I have no faith in vaccination I should therefore not have recommended it but it seems to satisfy them. I have had no pain in my back which makes me believe that the leaving off wine has been of service to me and my apples are still efficacious. The Bachelors Ball went off extremely well and there is to be a Race Ball on Monday next. I fear therefore our Preachers only labour in vain for they seem not to be listened to; however I go to the Lecture every Wednesday morning and I hope I shall profit by it. Trusting I shall have a good account soon I shall close this with kind regards to the Sollys also to your Neighbours and believe me my Dearest Sister with love to Mr. Rackett and you,
Your very Affecte.
F. Davis.

D-RAC/C/61. Letter from W. A. Miles to Rev. T. Rackett.

50, Judd Street,
Brunswick Square
March 23rd 1827.
Dear Sir,

119 Since Easter fell on April 15th in 1827, the dinner party described actually took place during Lent. (HSLD)

Waiting the turn of events I have removed to London and am now at the above address housed with Mrs. Miles – as yet I have nothing settled but thr' the interest of Mr. Caley I am in hopes of obtaining a temporary employment in the indexing of the Privy Council Papers – and in the Interim, I am transcribing a Chronicle of Stowe's[120] which is in the Harleian Collection – for Mr. Amgott – who is doubtless known to you. At first I found difficulty in deciphering them but the kindness of Mr. Beltz smoothed the Path and all is easy – How delighted & how happy I should have been if his Grace the Archbishop of Canterbury had thought proper to heed the application of Sir R..C. Hoare and that I had been appointed under Mr. Hawkins instead of Mr. Banwell (in) the new office. It is however otherwise ordained! and I sincerely regret that the important patronage of a Museum[121] is vested in the hands of one man who has so much to attend to, & whose patronage is so extensive that he would not loose much by resigning it to his Colleagues.

The noise and bustle of London is by no means congenial to my feelings and I sigh for the deepest solitudes – Give me a bleak tract of country and a spade in my hand in preference to all the splendour of the Metropolis! would to God that I had three hundred a year! I should devote my time to study and research – and I cannot but think that if my case were laid before his Majesty that such a pension would be granted to me.

I have met with curious Etymologies relative to our Purbeck names – which convince me more & more of the Phoenician colonists having there fixed their residence and even established their fire worship. Thus the required security, which neither their numbers nor their power could afford (a few defenceless men in intercourse with the rude erratic Hordes) was obtained by the mind subduing terrors of religion! The fire altar, hallowed & revered, would defend a Pass as effectively as an Army & such no doubt was the singular mount of Corfe, on which now stands in ruined splendour the fortress Walls of Men and haughty Barons. What a vast and noble ruin! Yet how little noticed! It is a subject on which the mind can never weary and as I carry it back to a holy purpose, of more intense interest it is to me. Nature has defended the coast by the chalk range, and only one spot is accessible – namely at Corfe – there is a Gap – Cor=aph the fire or the altar of the sun – on the high place – and when the encrimsoned flag of Victory floated over the Saxon Plunderers, their numbers great they trusted not to the Dominion of terror but depended upon sure ground Physical power & the Holy altar was made a strong fastness – But let me conclude – trusting that you will bear me still in mind – I remain

Dr. Sir Your oblig'd & devoted Servt.

W.A. Miles.

D-RAC/E/113. Letter from Dorothea, daughter of Rev. Thomas and Mrs. Rackett.

120 John Stowe (1525-1605) wrote a series of chronicles of the history of England. His manuscripts are now mainly in the Harleian Collection in the British Library. 'Mr Amgott' remains elusive; in 1810 there appears to have been one Thomas Amgott occupying a house in Downing Street.

121 Under the terms of its foundation in 1753, the British Museum was governed by a board of 25 trustees, chaired by the Archbishop of Canterbury, the Lord Chancellor and the Speaker of the House of Commons. The British Museum Act of 1963 did away with this.

Dear Papa & Mama
As we were out of paper I could not write before & only a few words as Mr. S. will take it to Lincoln with him and finish it there. In our drive yesterday we saw two most picturesque figures that I wished for Papa's pencil to sketch. A boy with a cask before him on a Donkey followed by a Woman in a red cloak and blue petticoat carrying an earthen vessel. They were in Norton Disney wood tapping the birch trees for wine.[122]

Having had occasion to write to Gower Street for some things I wanted Mary writes that she hopes we shall not be offended at her want of care for our things, and that I will intercede with you in her behalf that she may obtain forgiveness on promising most faithfully that she will never be guilty of the like fault again.

This is the first spring day we have had, and we must now garden as fast as we can. I received a very affectionate letter from Mrs. Wheler the other day, she seems pretty well and says Mrs. Tatt & herself will set off for Yorkshire on Monday next on a visit to the Miss Medhursts, they will pass the summer at the sea side. It was very unlucky that owing to the letter being left at the wrong house I did not get it in time to answer it before they left Kent so that I could not even make an appointment to meet them at Newark which place I suppose they will pass through.

(The next part of the letter is in Mr. Solly's writing. Ed.) Dorothea has been rather squeamish but being perfectly well in other respects. Our medical man prescribes nothing but palateable food, I have found perch boiled in the usual way with parsley roots seemed the best. It has agreed so well with her that she dines upon it to day for the third time. She does not agree with the doctors opinion as to the cause of this nausea but he is certainly right in his mode of treating it. I drive her about in a gig with a large lead. You must not take any notice in your answer of this information for otherwise she will insist upon being left to give an account of herself. I am busy with the search after our late servant, who has been allowed to remain at large in spite of the warrant I took out against him ....
Affectionately your
D.L.R.S.
Lincoln, 23 March 1827.

D-RAC/D/86. Letter from George Baker to Mrs. Rackett.

122 Birch sap thus drawn during the annual sap-flow in March can be fermented as a kind of beer. It is mentioned by John Evelyn in the 2nd. Edn. of *Sylva,* 1669-70, as one of the 'Treen Liquors' (i.e. made from trees). He advises the use of an auger rather than an incision as advocated by Sir Hugh Plat at an earlier date, and prefers the liquor drawn at the junction of trunk and branch, attributing an occult virtue to it. Evelyn states it was good for the kidneys, and gives a recipe for birch wine: a quart of honey to a gallon of sap boiled for almost an hour with a few cloves and a little Lemon peel. (HSLD)

Waterloo Hotel, Jermyn Street, 5 April 1827.
My dear Aunt,
You will perhaps be as much surprized by seeing the place whence I am writing as by the sight of my hand-writing which I am ashamed to say has become dreadfully scarce. Here we are & have been for about a week for the purpose of having our children looked at by those whose inspection was necessary to expand their growth in proper form viz dentists, corset makers, &c. &c. and the toils of farming and teaching & of expounding the law to the rustics being laid aside I resume my long neglected pen to tell you in the first place that as you do not farm, nor teach children, nor practice as a lawyer (though I make no doubt you & the Philosopher do that which is lawful and right) you may was well now and then indulge me with an account of yourselves; and in the next, what we have been doing and are going to do.

On Wednesday the 28th of March we packed ourselves about a post chaise Mary & the eldest girls being within it & my eldest boy & I on the Dickey & to London we came in spite of wind which was as boisterous as ever I experienced & as the surface of the ground was dry & loose I had my eyes Mcadamized and my nose salamandered on that day & on all the others we have been Gerrard's guests except that we sleep & breakfast here for his house is too full to furnish accommodation to any else of a corporeal nature besides its usual inhabitants.

We have been engaged pretty much by day & night in seeing sights – among those which I accompanied them in visiting were the Chinese Ladies – of whom I cannot attempt a description not having had an opportunity of satisfying myself with a proof that they are ladies at all – the natural characteristics which they exhibit to a superficial observer are a copper colored round face small eyes, snubby nose, thick lips, & very little feet and a dress which you would call beautiful because you are better able to appreciate the excellence of its materials than I am. They and their chinese uncle are like a group of figures on a saucer – and seemed very happy and contented and civil to us all. Besides these the children have been to panoramas &c. &c. and they are delighted with everything – On Saturday night we went to Drury Lane and saw the Slave, & X, Y, Z. Their musical force is good consisting of Miss Stevens, Braham, Madame Vestris & Liston is a host but the rest seemed very inferior gentry. – But perhaps I may be growing old & cynical. On Monday we went to Covent Garden and saw Oberon - & the Pantomime Mother Shipton – I thought Miss Paton pretty & a pretty singer but inferior to Miss Stevens – I believe the fashionable world are disposed to set her above her rival and there are different opinions of her beauty – My little girl Bessey was sick and obliged to leave the house at the beginning of the Pantomime & as I attended her saw little else of it than a very fine black cat. On Tuesday we went to the Opera La Vestale which comprized opera divertisment & ballet – No singers here equal to Catalani & Tramezzani though I like Caraderi. We have had a dinner party at Pall Mall on Friday last, & are to have another there to day & this is pretty well for one week & to morrow we hie away for St. Stephens. I find by the newspapers that you have discovered some burning mountains near Weymouth[123]. Has the Philosopher or have any of you explored it – let him beware of his predecessor Pliny's fate[124].

You know that Wheler has left his property to Jane for her life – than which he could not have done a more just or proper thing, - it is then to go to the Medlands & if they fail of producing issue it is to pass away to a youth of the name of Monteith – a legacy of £100 per annum to his mother instead of the use of Hall's place, & one of £100 (not per annum) to his sister is all he has done for those most connected with him by blood except indeed that John is to have the living of Harewood on the next vacancy when that happens, the present incumbent being 56 years old – I have not seen our friend Dr. Maton – He is too much in vogue to want a morning visit – I was grievously vexed at finding your house still deserted – if you can contrive to be so long out of London you may as well come to see us & our Railroad[125] will be something new to you. Mary desires her particular love to you both – in which she is most cordially joined by our very affc. Nephew G. Baker.
Give our loves to our Cousins if with you and also to Aunt Davis.

D-RAC/E/111. Letter from Thomas King to Thomas Rackett.

Windsor N.S.
12th May 1827
My dear Friend,
Some time ago I had the pleasure of receiving your kind letter of 19th October, but deferred answering it till I again heard from you upon the subject of a Nautical Table which I forwarded to you last autumn to be presented to the Society for the encouragement of the Arts, but from your silence I am afraid it has not reached you. The Table is very simple, it ascertains with expedition and accuracy (from the Log Book) the progress of the vessel. If it is your opinion that it may give my name any celebrity, or help to save it from oblivion, you of course will have great pleasure in telling me so, as I know your affection for me is little short of that of a Father.

Since I have commenced Farmer [sic] I have been for the most part in constant trouble and difficulties. This country is only fit for such as work themselves. The wages are thrice what they are at home, their diet more expensive and the market lower, besides the great distance the Farmers have to carry their produce. We have but one market in this province, most of the business is done by Barter and yet the servants and Tradesmen expect to be paid in cash. Now this is impossible from a

123 The allusion refers to the burning cliff at Ringstead, from which a vapour-like steam was seen to issue from several apertures and fissures in 1822. Observers noted similar occurrences at intervals up to and including 1827. (HSLD)

124 Pliny the elder was caught up in the eruption of Vesuvius in A.D.79 and died trying to rescue his friends at Stabiae.

125 To which Railroad Baker is referring is uncertain. The Stockton and Darlington railway was first opened for passengers on 27 Sept. 1825, but there was the Surrey iron railway worked by horses, first opened in 1801, from Wandsworth to Croydon. (HSLD)

private income. Then there is no subordination, hardly any skill or knowledge for most of the Emigrants are ignorant Irishmen just caught. Implements of husbandry badly constructed and enormously expensive. Blacksmith's bills intolerable – mine for last year upwards of £96!! Added to all this there is great jealousy of any person of consequence coming among them. You must be constantly on your guard to prevent them from over reaching you, and it is seldom if you appeal to the Law, or leave the matter to arbitration that you obtain redress.

You must wonder then if I have taken steps to relieve myself from such a state of things. I have leased the Farm, retaining the dwelling and ground about it, for seven years. The Tenant has the use of all my stock (after selling what he did not require) upwards of 300 sheep, 8 horses and about 12 cows and young stock, and my carts, waggons, ploughs, &c. I am to have one half of all the stock, produce &c. free of any expence. The Tenant is a skilfull Englishman, he is diligent, honest and sober, rare qualities with us. Taking one year with another, the advantages I shall possess, will be nearly equivalent to the interest of the money invested. Indeed double the money expended in Town would not give the comfort and respectability. The only difficulty I have now is to pay off my incumbrances which I am not without hope in doing. I can do little in the way of economy, for no person in my situation could live plainer than I have done since my residence in the Country.

About a twelve month ago I was put into the Commission, and in the performance of my duties I have met with much approbation. It will afford you much happiness to learn that I have become very religious. For the last year I have put myself entirely at the disposal of my Saviour (till then I have depended too much on myself). I have brought my temper under some control, have ceased to swear, and addressed my Maker morn and night, never omitting to pray for my dear friends to whom, through providence I am so much obligated. I beg your prayers, that I may continue firm in my resolutions, and that my faith and hope may gain in strength. How happy it would make me to see you all once more! The least encouragement would bring me to Spettisbury. You must grant me one favour, that of sitting for your miniatures to one of our best artists, I mean those of Mrs. R., Mrs. Solly & yourself. My Agent Greenwood &c. &c. will pay the expence. This indulgence you must not deny me, for my affection strengthens as the years increase. The more Knowledge I have of the world, the more do I appreciate your goodness to me, and the benevolence of your dispositions. I am now much of the world, but never have I met with your equal! If you are not saved, what will be the lot of mankind?

Had I been under a tutor of similar character mine would have been moulded upon it, and perhaps have realised your wishes in following your profession. But my disposition is a peculiar one, any tendency to harshness has always (one word illegible here. Ed.) my mind, excited my temper and thwarted the very object in view . Had I children never would I suffer them to be so degraded & abused as they are at Home. A different system is used on this side of the water, and greater progress no children can make. In process of time their superiority will be acknowledged. One of my wife's sons is now at our Windsor college, he is about 16 years old, has been there about twelve months, and is an excellent Greek & Latin scholar. There are about 25 or 30 in that

University from which they are fast supplying the learned professions of this Province. They are now about establishing another college in New Brunswick upon a more liberal footing. Ours excludes Dissenters. Our Bishop, Inglis, is a Native and educated here. If you make enquiry among your clerical brethren, for he has latterly been frequently in England, you will learn he has talents & character that would reflect honour in any country.

As this letter is intended for Mrs. Rackett, as well as yourself, I have now only to add how happy it will make me to have a few lines from her own hand, stating she is well, and that I am blessed with her affections. Mrs. Solly too, I hope will continue to think of me, if only for your sakes. God's blessing on you all, and confide in my sincerity when I say how truly I love you.

Your ever affectionate
Thomas King.

D-RAC/C/62. Letter from Thomas H. Bastard[126] to Rev. Thomas Rackett.

Charlton Augst. 5th 1827.
Dear Sir,
You will excuse my troubling you again respecting the Arms of Creech which if you have been able to procure should be glad to have as the Wadham folks are now about putting in another window in the Hall and would wish to introduce them in it with theirs _____ I have got an impression from a seal which I have no doubt is correct but cannot from the faintness of the engraving correctly make out the colours of the emblazoning ____ The Impression is the field Ermine but whether on black or the reverse cannot make out with a pale up the centre on which are three swords patee fitchee ______ Crest a Lion crowned holding a patee fitchee in the right paw or it may be a sword with a sort of Patee fitchee hilt _______ You will now be able to compare this with those you may have procured, but I have every reason to think the Impression I have is correct. I am just returned from the Assizes where I am sorry to say from the number of indictments for horse stealing that crime seems to be on the increase ______ but the Judges having been for some time inclined to try lenient punishment now find it necessary to let the law take its full force and one man a notorious thief is left for execution without hope of mercy and I understand that is to be the case where convicted on clear and good evidence _____ We have now to thank all Bountiful providence for a beautiful and luxuriant crop of corn and not doubt if we trust in him and do our duty he will add a fine time to take it and I will add that I hope the warmth of the season will force you into the country to enjoy the sight _____ Some of our neighbours who have been keeping in their wheat will now feel the consequences as well as in wool ___ I hope Mrs Rackett is better than when she left the

126 Descended from Thomas Bastard, brother of the architects who rebuilt Blandford Forum after the fire of 1731. Other local buildings are attributed to them, including Charlton Marshall church. This branch of the family settled in Charlton Marshall and lived there for several generations.

country & to whom I beg my best respects and believe me to be
Dear Sir
Yours very Sincerely
Th. H. Bastard.

D-RAC/C/61. Letter from W.A. Miles to Rev. T. Rackett at Blackden Cottage, Newark, from the Post Office, Doncaster.

Sunday morning (1827)
Dear Sir,
I have been at the pains & the expence to travel here in order to pass a month with a friend and as I had anticipated a pleasure in taking him by surprize, imprudently I did not ascertain if he were at his seat near here, & on my arrival I find he has gone upon an antiquarian tour to visit the round Towers in Ireland & thus am I miserably disappointed & shall return to Town long before my holidays are expired. I have a month from the Museum & really a little country air to relieve the London Smoke is highly acceptable. On Tuesday I intended paying my respects to the venerable Keep at Coningsbury Castle[127] which King in his Mon. Ant.[128] discourses on, and his learned observations will be doubly relished on re-perusal after having visited the relics. There are barrows near it, & I shall be almost tempted to try one. Mr. King if I remember right stamps it as a Phoenician relic, what a pleasure if I should find only but a particle of the Kimmeridge coal. – a fragment – a mite of it!

I fear the distance is too far from you to join me in the excursion – the castle is only five miles from here - & the Stamford two-horse coach passes thr' Newark every day about 12 & you arrive here at 6 p.m. The coach which comes to the Saracen's head is an opposition concern & they will bring you almost for the sake of your company – When shall I have the pleasure of again exploring with such warm & indefatigable friends as Mr. & Mrs. Solly? – If is it likely that I may be favoured with your Company I will defer my trip to Coningsbury for a day – but I am anxious to leave here by friday - as my expences are heavy being in Lodgings.

The friend whom I came to see is Godfrey Higgins[129] of Skellow Grange the Author of that luminous work on the *Celtic Druids* which I had the pleasure of shewing to you.

I think much may be discovered at Doncaster – but horse racing is all the theme here - & I suspect the Doncastrians like base idolaters of old, worship false images in

127 Conisbrough Castle is dominated by a great cylindrical and buttressed keep, erected in the 1170s or 1180s. It was the inspiration for Scott's *Ivanhoe*, published in 1819. Skellow is a village north-east of Doncaster.

128 Edward King (1735-1807), *Munimenta Antiqua*, 4vols, 1799-1806.

129 Godfrey Higgins (1772-1833), historian and antiquarian. He was appointed 'Chosen Chief' of the Order of Druids founded by John Totland in 1717. He devoted his life to the association of Biblical narrative with world religions. *The Celtic Druids* was published in three parts between 1827 and 1829.

the hearts - & that the racehorse is to them as the Cat, the Bull, or the Ibis was to the Egyptians & Indeed I have actually seen some of the idolaters wearing a small Deity of a race horse at full gallop upon their chests fastening their neckcloths to their shirts, after the manner of our Broaches – but I fear those models were but the images of their Deity of the Horse – I have read of Heliopolis & I should propose that the name of Doncaster be changed to that of Hippopolis – at once classical & significant.

Beds during the race week 7 & 8 guineas a week – they actually charge me 2/- a pound for fresh Butter – I cannot stand this place – I must to London – I shall open my mouth, inhale a last gasp of pure delicious fragrant country air and hie away to my Museum room.

As I am compelled to study oeconomy I fear that I shall proceed directly up to London per coach & not stop at Newark – as I intended – by breaking the Journey & sleeping at Stamford – I should wish however to have the pleasure of your society to relate to you my fortunes and my sorrows – in both of which I know that you rejoice & participate – Pray remember me most sincerely & most kindly to Mr. & Mrs. Solly – as also to Mrs. Rackett, Believe me to be Dr. Sir most truly & sincerely your faithful
W.A.M.

D-RAC/C/47. Letter from Charles St. Barbe to Rev. T. Rackett.

Lymington
31. Jan 1828
My Dear Sir,
I am much obliged to you for your entertaining letter of the 25th. As I have not recovered my Antiquarian plates, I am anxious to replace them by purchasing them of the Society which I will trouble you to do for me and also to take up the Vol. or pt. of the Archd. which as it contains the notice of the Beacon Crest at Sopley I wish to peruse – If you will give the Librarian his fee (which by the by I think is too great a tax on the Members & ought to be discontinued) I shall be much obliged to you – and on your sending the prints & book to Mrs. Combe in Caroline Street with a note of the disbursement she will repay you, having my directions so to do. I have sent you the sword; I shall be happy to hear that it is worthy of a place in Dr. Meyricks collection;[130] and the first time I go on tour I will endeavour to accept his invitation to Cadogan Place.

You appear to have many interesting novelties, the Steam carriage[131] will

130 Samuel Rush Meyrick (1783-1848) collector of antique arms and armour. In 1824 he published *A Critical Enquiry into Antient Armour.* In 1828 he built Goodrich Court where he established a huge armoury. He was employed to reorganize the armouries at the Tower of London and Windsor Castle. His collection was dispersed after his death, although parts are in the British Museum and the Wallace Collection.

131 Not having come across any reference to this Steam carriage, it is assumed that Rackett had been toying with such a notion, or even making experiments. In 1825 Goldsworthy Gurney produced steam carriages in his workshops in London. One successfully ran from London to

astound us Country folks, should it be adopted for a long journey, but I imagine it must first be tried in the neighbourhood of the metropolis – for a while.

Having taken a more desirable house than my present, and on the other side of the Street looking to the sea, we are very busy planning for a removal at Lady Day – we hope you will come and see us this summer, and enjoy the view from the lawn behind it.

With compliments to the Ladies, Mr. Solly & a kiss from her Godmother to the little Francesca Thomasina,

I remain very truly, my Dear sir, Your's C. St. Barbe.

D-RAC/C/61. Letter from W.A. Miles to Rev. T. Rackett.

Winchester Street,
Sarum, May 21. 1828.
Dear Sir,

Dorsetshire has such charms for me, that I could not resist the temptation of going to Dorchester, and visiting Maiden Castle, and subsequently opening a barrow. – Stonehenge is a most extraordinary remain but I think Maiden Castle especially wonderful – the Western Entrance is the finest specimen of Military skill, that in my opinion can exist – and the constructors of such a fortress, must have been a more polished race than we are led to suppose. I was particularly struck, with the terrace formed on the south western side of the second escarpment which doubtless you have observed – this terrace overlooks an inferior Bank work and immediately behind this terrace is a platform of considerable extent running along the inner side of the trench, so that the upper part of the Bank, forms a Breast work to those who stand upon the Platform immediately behind the terrace, unseen by those who stand on the outer Bank – in the centre of this terrace, stands a small mound, and here, in all probability stood the Castle Chief, when holding Parley with his Foe – apparently unguarded, but in whose rear, hid from sight, by the Breast-work, stood thousands ready to protect him from any treacherous effort of the enemy – I found several pieces of Ancient Pottery, precisely similar in material, & ornament, to the black specimens of Kimmeridge!

I also found beneath the soil, intermixed with the Pottery, two fragments of Purbeck stone, evidently shaped – This will sanction an idea that Maiden Castle existed when a settlement existed at Kimmeridge and I am now all anxiety to open a Barrow near the Camp, as its contents may throw a new light upon the former Race who used this Camp – What is there not to be expected in Dorset – Wales, Cornwall & Mona,[132] may contain more Druidical remains but, in Wales & Mona, they are comparatively modern to the Dorset relics – The Camps of Dorset & other remains, were constructed

---

Bath and back, but public reluctance to use this apparently dangerous machine resulted in the failure of his business. In Bundle 144[D-RAC/H/144] in the Dorset Record Office, document (v) there is a diagram entitled 'Mr. Rackett's Boiler'. This however, has no date. (HSLD)

132 *Mona Insula* is the Roman name for the Isle of Anglesey.

when the Briton was free & not forced into the Mountain Posts as in Wales – a Grecian or a Phoenician colony has existed at Kimmeridge, Druidism is allowed to have been imported by the Phoenicians, the altars of Dorset are all near the sea, & it is but fair to conclude (if the introductions of an established worship ameliorates mankind), that this county and Cornwall were the first which felt the influence of Druidism & consequently, Government.

The Barrow which I explored was in a field near where the Turnpike Gate stood at Dewlish, about 1½ or two miles west of Milbourne – it was constructed as follows, the superstructure was Earth, below which we came to a very tenacious dark coloured clay about 2 feet in thickness and beneath this there was a Heap of flints (in the centre) placed very compact & formed like an oven and in the native Chalk was cut a cist, whose mouth was considerably less than the interior of the Chamber – this contained the bones of a young Person, as is evident by the Jaw bone which I have in my possession – From the minor Barrows which I have explored, it appears to me that the Ashes of children were deposited under smaller Tumuli – I have observed that certain Bones are frequently much heavier that can naturally be accounted for, and I should wish to learn why this extreme weight occurs. Can you put me in the way of ascertaining this curious point – an analysis would detect it – it has occured to me whether these bones, generally being the complete bones of the tibia, ulna &c., may not have commenced a transition to a state of stone. Sir R.C. Hoare is at present from home, and my work of Deverell[133] is standing still, as he [has] kindly undertaken to revise my proof sheets – In the Interim trusting that you may bear me in mind, should any opportunity occur for my advantage, I remain with respectful compliments to the Ladies. Dr. Sir.

Most Sincerely, Your obliged
Will. Aug. Miles.
P.S. Allow me to ask if you have heard from Mr. Cayler.

D-RAC/E/102. Letter from Charles Hatchett to Mr. & Mrs. Th. Rackett.

Belle View House, Chelsea
Oct. 31. 1828.
My dear Mr. and Mrs. Rackett,
I thank both of you for your kind letter which came to my hands on our return not from Lincolnshire but from a coasting tour. The fact is that the bad weather during the summer had caused so many blue devils to dance before the eyes of the farmers that I was advised not to put myself in the way of their solicitations which could not be granted with any degree of prudence, whilst to reject them would perhaps have been somewhat painful. As therefore my presence was not absolutely required, I did not go but made a tour with Mrs. Hatchett to Margate, Broadstairs, Ramsgate, Dover

133 The Deverel Barrow was almost totally excavated by Miles in 1824. It is a bowl barrow, part of a scheduled Bronze Age long barrow cemetery on Deverel Down in Milborne St Andrew.

and Hastings. A good many years have elapsed since I visited any of these places excepting Hastings, and I particularly wished to be at Margate on a Saturday when the grand importation of men, women and children takes place from London by the Steam Vessels[134] of which no less than five arrived when we were there. Dover is beginning to become a fashionable bathing place, and if the new buildings continue to increase I have no doubt that it will prove a successful Rival to Brighton and the other Places. The spirit of migration seems to have been uncommonly powerful in this year, almost everybody has felt its influence (even Mrs. Rackett has not escaped) and the consequence of Water Wagtailish propensities caused all the places which we visited to be uncomfortably full, so that at times we found difficulty in obtaining accommodations. Another annoyance arose from the execrable quality of the Butter and Bread, the first being like coagulated Lamp Oil, the second like Glazier's Putty! Strange to say, that when I complained of the Butter the constant answer was "Very sorry indeed Sir, but we really at present have nothing but Country Butter though we hope to be able tomorrow to get some from London"!!!! So that it would seem as if all the principal Dairies were in London! What the Devil is the meaning of this !!? It approaches to some of the statements in that Wild Work the *Mummy*[135], which I suppose you have read. In the year 2126 as stated in that Book all Letters were sent to their respective destinations by Post Office Bullets, which by a certain whizzing noise gave People notice to get out of their way while they were in transitn [sic]. The Farming Bailiff also says to his Master "Sir, the meadows younder are too dry, and the grass begins to be parched, do you wish me to get out the Electrical Machine and make a few showers?" Speaking of the *Mummy* puts me in mind of a much superior work, I mean *Salathiel*[136], the Author (a man of acknowledged abilities) is the Rev. J. Croly, and he is not thought to have diminished his reputation by this book The descriptive scenery is highly vivid, and well it may be so considering the Legend of the Wandering Jew is the basis of the work and therefore the scope of him and variety of the country afford a most extensive range to the imaginative powers of the Author. If the Ladies wish to read a new Novel, I recommend *Pelham*[137]. We hope to go to Brighton about the 10th of November previous to which if there is anything I can do for either of you have the goodness to write to me. The last Dividends (£215.12.6.) I have paid to Mr. Racketts account at Cocks and Biddulphs immediately on receiving your letter on the 15th August. At present the only Dividend due is that of Ten Pounds ten shillings on the 600 three and a half per cents. Let me know if you wish it to be sent to you. Mrs Hatchett joins me in kind regards to you and also to Mr. & Mrs. Solly who with little Thomasina we hope are quite well.

And I am, Dear Mr. & Mrs. Rackett,
Most truly yours
Chas. Hatchett.

134 The Margate Steam Packet Company was established in 1815 using wooden paddle boats.
135 *The Mummy! A tale of the Twenty-Second Century*, by Jane Webb, 1827.
136 *Salathiel*, by Rev. George Croly (1780-1860).
137 *Pelham*, by Edward Bulwer Lytton, 1828.

D-RAC/C/66. Letter to Rev. Th. Rackett from Bishop of Bristol.

College, Durham, Nov. 10. 1828
Sir,
It has been stated to me, though perhaps not altogether upon such authority as I can depend, that there is a great complaint amongst your Parishioners at Charlton & Spettisbury, that you are never at home, and that your Curate lives at Blandford, that all the children attend at a large Meeting house as there is no Church School in the Parish, & that many converts are made to the Nunnery & Catholic Chapel. I shall be happy to receive a letter from you upon these subjects. By your Parochial return there was some doubt as to residence.
I am Sir,
Your obt. Friend & Brother
R. Bristol[138].

Ditto, to Th. Rackett from Bishop of Bristol.

College, Durham, Nov. 20 1828
Revd. Sir,
I am obliged to you for your prompt reply to my enquiries relative to your Parishes and I am very happy to find that you are able to refute so satisfactorily many of the insinuations that had been thrown out respecting the state of Spettisbury & Charlton. I should be sorry to dwell more at length upon the charges which I allude to as coming from such authority as I could not entirely depend upon, and I trust that you will not suppose I have allowed them to leave any unjust impression upon my mind. Permit me to suggest the propriety of making every exertion to counteract the baneful influence of the Roman Catholic Religion in your neighbourhood and of course encouraging the children of the Dissenters as much as possible to attend your church – I rejoice that you have such a well endowed school at Spettisbury. If you had made known to me the cause of your absence from your Parish beyond the time allowed by Law, I should have had no difficulty in granting a License for a few weeks.
I remain
Revd. Sir,
Yr. faithful Friend & Brother
R. Bristol.

Ditto. From 36 Gt. Geo. St. March 24 1829.

Revd. Sir,
I am obliged to you for your letter which arrived very opportunely and enabled me to shew, with some other papers in my possession, that the Marquis of Lansdowne had greatly misrepresented your case. I am sorry that you should have been subjected to

138 Robert Gray (1762-1834), Bishop of Bristol from 1827 until his death in 1834.

any unjust reflections, and have little doubt but that in a short time the impression will be counteracted. I am,
Revd. Sir,
Your faithful friend & Brother
R. Bristol.

D-RAC/C/66. Letter to Rev. Th. Rackett from Bishop of Bristol. Cheltenham Jy. 12. 1829

Revd. Sir,
It is with much regret that I feel myself compelled to inform you that complaints are again transmitted to me which I must request your serous attention. It is alleged in a letter which I have recently received "That you scarcely ever reside, that there is no church school & that a large Catholic Church is now building in your Parish" etc. Allow me to express the hope that the imputation of non Residence may not be substantiated, that you will endeavour to establish and effectively keep up a well regulated school which surrounded as you are must be of particular importance. I feel every disposition to give you credit for the past intentions but circumstanced as you are and [sic] particular circumspection and exertions are requisite.

If you require a Trustee for your School there would I consider be strong grounds for an application to the National Society. Where does your Curate at present reside. I hope to have the pleasure of seeing you in Dorchester this autumn.
I remain, Revd. Sir,
Your faith. friend and Brother
R. Bristol

Copy of an excerpt from The Times, March 20, 1829.
"The Marquis of Lansdowne agreed (with the Bishop of Bristol) that it was very essential to provide for the security of the established church; but that this would be done in the most efficient manner by the regular discharge of their duties by resident clergymen. This (Gloucester) petition came from a district in which the Catholic religion did not only exist, but had been on the increase, and he was happy to have the opportunity of stating, in the presence of the house, and of the right rev. prelate, an instance of highly culpable conduct respecting the discharge of clerical duties which was much more likely to produce injury to the established church than any measure which could proceed from the legislature. In a part of the County of Dorset which was, he believed, in the Diocese of the right rev. prelate, there had been for many years a nunnery, in which there were a great number of Catholic ladies remarkable for their zeal for the religion they professed. The part of Dorsetshire to which he alluded consisted of two villages, and during the whole of that time the nunnery existed, though the living worth 750L a year, there had never been a resident clergyman there. (Hear, hear). The living, to which another living was attached, was the living at Spettisbury, for which the rector had resided in London for 30 years,

during which time there had not been even a resident curate in the place. Now, if the Catholic religion had increased there, let him not hear it said that it was owing to the encroaching spirit of that religion, but let it be attributed to the real cause – the want of efficient discharge of clerical duties on the spot by a resident clergyman ..."

D-RAC/C/66. Draft of a letter from The Rev. Th. Rackett to the Bishop of Bristol. No date (but c. 22 March 1829)[139]

My Lord,

Having read this day in the report of Thursday's debate in the H. of Lords an accusation of culpable negligence on the part of the Rector of Spettisbury, in the Marquess of Lansdowne's speech, I loose no time in submitting to your Lordship the following reply.

It is stated by the noble Marquess that for the last 30 years I have resided in London and have not even had a resident Curate – I positively assert that I have resided in my rectorial house at Spettisbury every year during the last 40 years, although I will readily admit that some circumstances of a private domestic nature have at various times during that period occasioned my temporary absence beyond the period allowed by Law. Such circumstances were always stated to your Lordship's predecessors and never on any occasion found to be unreasonable.

My Curate who could not be placed in the Parsonage House occupied by myself has always resided a mile and a half from my Parish and I challenge even the "good authority" from which the Marquess professed to derive his information to produce a single instance of neglect of duty or complaint during the whole period of my incumbency. With respect to the culpable negligence with which I am accused as respecting the Convent of Augustine Nuns[140] in Spettisbury. I will admit, with his Lordship the great respectability of the members of that religious establishment. I will also admit their zeal, for there are at this moment preparations making for enlarging their Chapel. I beg however to call your Lordship's attention to the following fact. The number of families in S. is 108 out of which 5 or 3 of the families are connected with the Convent and were always so. There remain 2 families and 6 individuals who

139 It was Rackett's misfortune that this charge of non-residence, which was alleged to have allowed the rise of Catholicism in his parish, should have been raised just as the House of Lords was debating the Catholic Emancipation Bill. The Bill aroused strong feelings in the country and the debates were followed closely by all the leading newspapers. Lord Lansdowne used the case as an example of the complacency of the established church and the newspapers seized on it. Before long, everyone knew the story of the absentee clergyman of Spetisbury. This episode is investigated fully by G.J. Davies in 'Was Thomas Rackett guilty of absenteeism?' in *Somerset and Dorset Notes and Queries*, Vol. XXXV, Pt. 356, September 2002, Pp. 156-165.

140 Spetisbury House was acquired in 1800 by an exiled community of Augustinian nuns from the convent of St. Ursula in Louvain, Belgium. The new convent was dedicated to St. Monica and seems to have housed 30-35 sisters. They converted the stables into a boarding school for 40 young ladies which provided the convent with an income. In 1822 they opened a school for poor girls from the village.

have been induced to embrace the C. religion. So much for the increase of Catholics in Spettisbury. For other proofs to repel the charge of negligence and abandonment of duty I must refer to a statement I lately remitted to your Lordship respecting the number of children educated at my expence and my exertions for the recovery of an endowed school in the Parish of Spettisbury. I deny therefore the whole of the charge, I deny that I have been for 30 years resident in London. I deny that the number of Catholic proselytes has been owing to the Rector's abandonment of his duty and I trust that the charge of negligence and abandonment of duty cannot in any shape be proved against him. Had the Noble Marquess directed his inquiries through the medium of his family connections in Dorsetshire, or of his most respectable friend, Mr. O. of M. Critchill[141], his information would have been more accurate and his censure less severe.

Under these grave and weighty charges it is a consolation to me, and I think a sufficient refutation of them to reflect that during my residence (I repeat the word) here for nearly half a century I have enjoyed the friendship favour and countenances of many of the most distinguished characters, both of the clergy and laity in this County. I am ready to state to your Lordship any further particulars you may think it necessary or advisable to call for.

The friendship I have formed with some and the favoured countenance I have recvd. from many of the most distinguished and worthy characters among the clergy and laity in all parts of the County during a residence of nearly half a century as it completely refutes the charge of being a non resident, is a source of great consolation to me under the circumstance of being singled out form the whole body of the clergy to be made the object of a serious, grave and .... heavy accusation before Parliament. (unsigned)

D-RAC/E/107. John Knowles to Rev. T. Rackett

Revd. Dear Sir,

I have just received your kind letter with the draught for £10.5.0. which I shall apply as you have pointed out. The last time I had the pleasure to see you were at fault respecting the passage, "the poet's eye &c." I have found it as a speech of Hippolital in the "*Midsummer Night's Dream*" Act 5, Scene 1st. I am much obliged to you for the offer of the apples, it would be only to deprive some other friend of them, for I neither eat them in pies, puddings or their native state. I am however equally favoured by your kind offer. A journey into Dorsetshire would be a thing of all others that I should like, but I am pretty certain that I cannot leave London this year, I have at present carpenters, painters and upholsterers in my house, you know that I am somewhat of a prig in my house appearing clean and neat, and I cannot leave these workmen to themselves, it would cause their bills to be double. The sale of Mr. Barrett's furniture

141 Almost certainly Mr. Oakden [Okeden] of Moor Crichel. (HSLD). The Okeden family acquired property in Moor Crichel by marriage in the late 17th century.

at Stockwell was completed on Monday, independently of the articles bought in, the furniture brought in a little more than £1,000. The pictures which I value at about £1,800 are in Mr. Christie's Ware-rooms[142]. I shall be truly glad when our trust terminates.

The life of Fuseli[143] is completed, in fact after you had the goodness to look over it, I was perfectly satisfied; I mean it is completed if the quarrel with the Rev. I. Bromley is omitted.

Sir Thomas Lawrence called upon me one evening last week and insisted on taking it with him, to this I had no objection for I can either adopt or reject any emendation of his, and it is to my interest that it should appear as perfect as it can be made.

I beg my kindest compts. to Mrs. Rackett. It will give me pleasure to see Mr. & Mrs. Solly in London. The flags in your picture are those of Burgundy, I find exactly the same in a French marine dictionary published 1727 and in them is placed "Bourgondieu"

Mr. Jones sold me a little picture of shipping last week, I believe by Monamy[144] "firing the evening gun", it has all the accuracy but not the charm of the younger Vanderveldt. They have published a memoir of Fuseli in the Imperial Magazine[145] for the month, and stolen my portrait, this they must have got from Mr. Hammond who was allowed by me to copy it. I am Revd. Dear Sir,
Your faithful friend and devoted Servt.
John Knowles,
1st Oct. 1829.

D-RAC/D/88. Letter from Mrs. Elizabeth Taylor nee Baker, afterwards Mrs. Munro, to Mrs. Rackett, her Aunt.

Castle, Cape Town
Dec. 9th 1829
My ever dear Aunt,
It is now nearly two months since we landed – and not one letter have I had from my dear family. I will however fervently hope that all may be as well as I wish them. I write to you my dear aunt by the first Mail which sailed from hence after our arrival – and having been sometime longer here now I can write with more decision as to the chances of our liking this Station - which with the sad drawback of being so very

142 Founded in 1766 by James Christie the auction house now trades as Christie, Manson and Woods.

143 Johann Heinrich Füssli (1741 -1825, known as Henry Fuseli, was a Swiss painter who spent most of his life in Britain. His close friend John Knowles (1781-1841) was his executor and published his biography in 1831.

144 Peter Monamy (1670-1749) Marine Painter. (HSLD)

145 The *Imperial Magazine and Monthly Record*, published by Samuel Drew. It covered religious, philosophical, historical, topographical and biographical subjects

far distant from all our dear Relations and Friends in England – I think will prove a satisfactory tho' by no means a cheap Sejour for our five years tour of Duty – one of which will end on the 6th of next month as it will then be one year since Munro received orders to come hither – I mentioned in my letter that you would meet with every detail of this Colony, a good description of Cape Town in a small octavo work of one Volume written by Mr. Wilberforce Bird and entitled the "State of the Cape of Good Hope" – in 1822 - sold by John Murray, Albemarle Street, London – the price 12s. – Mr. Bird has been a resident in this Colony for many years – and is called the Macenas of the Cape – Our House is small – but pleasantly situated – being so close to the Bay – that we can see any ship that comes in – We have a little garden which so totally neglected by our predecessor Col. Casey that it will this year produce only grapes and figs – Geraniums and weeks are growing in equal luxuriance over the chief part of it – but after the hot season I hope it will be made productive of more useful articles – This and the two following months form the hottest parts of the year – but as there are usually intervals of cool days we hope to remain at the Fort – instead of doing as most people do by moving into the Country – where the air is often degrees cooler than here – There is no such thing as furnished lodging – so every person that goes must take all their furniture – which as we are only just settled would be to us a formidable effort.

The rix daller/eighteen penny current coin/ is the coin of the Country – and the average charge for a most uncomfortable country Residence is from one hundred and fifty – to two hundred rix dallers per month – unfurnished, and with a stipulation that it must be hired for four or five months. At the time the thermometer is 75 in the shade in our dining room- We are all well in health – excepting my dear Catherine – who has not I fear even yet recovered the effects of her voyage – As yet we have not had any intelligence of Mr. Dickson not that we expect it for several months as he will not be aware for some time of our arrival at the Cape – I have met with the Daughter of my Son Charles's Lt. Col. Fitzgerald of the 20th Foot. She is married to Mr. Arbuthnot – they came to the Cape for her husband's health – She gratified me by speaking in the highest terms of my beloved Son – Who is much esteemed by her father Col. Fitzgerald – and is now Brigade Major at [illegible word here. Ed.] – My other dear Boy John who is in the 19th Light Infantry will soon be returning to England [illegible word here. Ed.] an unattached Company. – Our Society here is chiefly Military – I did hear from Col. Boyce/whom I met at / That the Grandson of your Friend Lady Coventry was at the Cape – by name Capt. Cotton – and I have enquired from him – but if in this Colony he must be at the Frontier/ about 500 miles from here as no such person is in this Garrison – I have had two little Musical parties and dances which gave so much satisfaction to my guests that I should have requested Capt. Cotton to have made one of the number had he been here-

I wish I could draw to give you a sketch of the Bullock teams, - and their black drivers, Which are really very picturesque. The teams often consist of eighteen or twenty Bullocks harnessed two abreast – they bring pipes of wine from the interior – and poor little Slave Boy runs before to guide them. The Houses in Cape Town are usually of white stone – and very large – The dress and appearance of the Dutch inhabitants are very like ourselves. We have dined with Col. & Lady Mary Fitzroy. She is sister to the present Duke of Richmond, and is very much liked at the Cape. She lent us the following to us new books – *Devereux*[146] by the Author of *Pelham* – *The Chelsea Pensioners*[147] – and *Tales of the Wars of our Times*[148] all of them worth reading.

Tomorrow we are going to dine at Government house – when I shall probably have Lady Frances Cole – and her sister Lady Catherine Bell sing Duets – and I shall think of Miss Davis who was I believe their Instructress, I rather dread the Day – as you know my dear Aunt I never like grand or formal meetings – but so it must be – I must now say how anxious I am to hear of you all – and my dear Aunt Davis – together with Dorothea and little Thom-

This is my dear Bro. George's birthday. I continually think of you all, and never shall I forget your great kindness to me and mine – Nath. and R. are both well – United to all,
Your Niece.

D-RAC/E/102. Letter from Charles Hatchet to Rev. Th. Rackett.

Brighton,
63 Regency Square,
Feb. 1. 1830.
Dear Rackett,
Your letter has given great pleasure to me and my wife by the good account of the health of all you at Spettisbury notwithstanding the extreme severity of the weather which in many places has caused much illness and great mortality. I never suffered so much from cold at this place until now, and have wished myself at home where my house is warmed by a stove and air flues. As to the warm sea breezes which you talk of, they (for this winter at least) only have existed in imagination, for we have been pierced with the North East wind, and are at this moment wrapped up in the Frost and Snow. In spite of all this Brighton has been very full of company and much too gay and too fine; I liked this much better ten years ago than I do now, for the life led here is precisely the same as in London, People send their Services of Plate and their whole establishment of servants, to which they even make occasional additions, for instance the Marchioness of Downshire lately gave a dinner to a Party of twenty and a Ball and supper the same evening to a party of fifty, to prepare which, she employed seven superior Men Cooks, namely her own, and another Frenchman resident here with the addition of five more from London, the number I suppose being in allusion to the Seven Wise Men of Greece or of Grease. The rent of furnished Houses in good situations is very high. I am paying twelve Guineas per week, but many are let at 14.16.18 or 20 Guineas a week. Whilst here we visited Tim and his family who have

146 *Devereux* (1829) and *Pelham* (1828), by Edward Bulwer Lytton (1803-1873)

147 By Rev. George Robert Gleig (1796-1888), chaplain to the Chelsea Hospital.

148 By Joseph Moyle Sherer (1789–1869), a British army officer, traveller and writer.

but lately left Brighton. What a state the Book Trade is in! An Eminent Bookseller lately wrote to me to offer a Subscriber's large paper copy (only 50 having been printed) of Caley & Ellis's Edition of Dugdale's *Monasticon* proof Plates and in 51 parts so that probably one part more will complete this Magnificent work. The cost to the Subscriber has been £269.15.0., and the sum asked of me was £75, but having just then returned 15 per cent to my Lincolnshire Tenants on old Rents which have not been raised for the last 22 years was quite sufficient for me to decline the offer.

Books are now terribly depreciated, and yet people are every day selling their Libraries. I am sorry and surprised to learn that Sir George Rose[149] is going to sell that fine Library at Cuffnells[150] which was formed by Lord Marchmont[151] (the friend of Pope) and left by Lord M. to the late Mr. Rose.

Sir Humphry Davy's posthumous work (entitled *Consolation in Travel*[152]) has just been published by Murray. I have not yet seen it, but a friend who has read it considers it upon the whole to be but flimsy and a sort of Medley which had better have remained in Manuscript. Some of the vagaries in it are however described to be original and amusing. My correspondent says "If I understand him rightly" the human soul is to migrate through the Planets (excepting through Mercury and Venus which are inhabited by more degraded Beings than those on Earth) and in each to receive accessions of perfection until fitted for the Cometary system, where it becomes attached to a Cherubim's form, and ultimately becomes so refined and sublimed as to be fit for its ultimate and highest destination." The inhabitants of Saturn are described as first rate Philosophers; in person they resemble sky blue Walrus's, very transparent, and having proposces like Elephants.

Dr. Paris[153] is writing Davy's Life in Quarto; and More has just published his Life of Lord Byron[154] which everybody reads, and with which everybody is dissatisfied. It is really too bad of them to drag their deceased friends with their living connections before the Public in order to put money into their own Pockets. It is said that Sir Thomas Lawrence's[155] professional income was from 15 to 20,000 per annum, and yet his debts are reported to be the amount of £80,000 or more. It is supposed that his unfinished pictures will cause much litigation.

Here and I believe in all the towns on the Coast Placards are put up offering £500 reward for the apprehension of Keith[156] the man who carried off 2804 Gold Blanks

149 Sir George Henry Rose, diplomatist and miscellaneous writer, 1771-1855. (HSLD)
150 Cuffnells was a large house on the outskirts of Lyndhurst. It was purchased in 1784 by George Rose.
151 Hugh Hume-Campbell, 3rd Earl of Marchmont (1708-1794)
152 *Consolations in Travel or The Last Days of a Philosopher*, said to have become a staple of both scientific and family libraries for several decades after its publication in 1830.
153 John Ayrton Paris (1785-1856) was a Fellow of the Royal Society, and for the last 12 years of his life President of the Royal College of Physicians.
154 Thomas Moore (1779-1852) was an Irish poet, appointed by Byron as his literary executor with instructions to publish his memoirs. Instead he destroyed them at the family's behest, but published the *Letters and Journals of Lord Byron* in 1830.
155 Sir Thomas Lawrence (1769-1830), leading English portrait painter.
156 George Keith, an employee in the moneyer's department at the Royal Mint, was entrusted

from the Royal Mint; he is supposed however to be concealed in London, as to the property there is but little chance of recovering any part of it, and if not recovered, the loss must be made good by the six moneyers, each of whom will have to pay £464.13.4. exclusive of all the expense they have been at in endeavouring to catch him.

It is our intention to leave this place for Chelsea on the 20th of this month, and in the course of the following week I hope to visit the Bank and receive Dividends which are due. I shall therefore be glad to receive a letter from you or Mrs. Rackett at that time to say what is to be done with her money and also to acquaint me with the name and description and place of residence of her third Trustee, so that I may when I go into the City be enabled to transfer the different Stocks into the names of the New Trust, and you will observe that as there are two separate accounts in the Consols and two separate accounts in the 3½ per Cents one of each of these must have the name of the third Trustee added to those of myself and Mr. Davis. You and Mrs. Rackett will therefore inform me which of the accounts in the Consols and which of the accounts in the 3&½ per Cents is to stand with the three names.

A Lady has just given me the enclosed lines which I have inclosed as I think Mrs. Rackett will be amused by them, I do not know who has written them but they give a true picture of much that passes here.

Give our best regards to Mrs. R. and to Mr. & Mrs. Solly, and love to little Thomasine[157], and believe me,
Yours most truly,
Chas. Hatchett.

D-RAC/E/113. Letter from Dorothea & Samuel Solly to Rev. T. & Mrs. Rackett.

Morton, August 1830.
Dear P., M.,
At the present moment Mr. Smith has great reason to congratulate himself, but though he was tired of his Spettisbury farms he seems to find it a difficult matter to know what to do with himself. George wished him to try a London life but he soon found that would not do, and if he engages deeply in farming at Goldicut[158] he will probably be worse off than if he had kept Spettisbury, which I always supposed he kept in his own hands only because he could not get a tenant at a rent proportionable to the price he had paid for it; according to the present rent it costs Mr. Drax[159] forty years purchase, but it might to [sic] let for one half more, which would make the price not more than

on 16 January 1830 with conveying gold blanks to be stamped. He took half of them, but never returned. A reward of £100 was offered for his apprehension and a further £300 for recovery of the property.

157 Frances Thomasine Langford Solly, daughter of Samuel and Dorothea Solly, was baptized at Swinderby in Lincolnshire in 1827.

158 Coldicote Farm, Moreton-in-Marsh (Glos.)

159 The Drax family resided at Charborough Park and had extensive estates in Dorset. In 1830 the head of the family was John Samuel Wanley Sawbridge Erle Drax.

twenty five or twenty six years purchase.

According to the tythe paid you by Mr. Smith, his farms ought to be worth twenty eight shillings per acre, and I hope your tythe for this year will prove they are worth this rent, but although they are let for twenty shillings I do not think the price paid for them by Mr. Drax which is more than forty guineas per acre, extravagantly dear.

I should think it is a good investment for money in the funds because I think they must fall considerably if any commotion takes place in Spain, Italy or the Netherlands, but without the assistance of a War Expenditure, rents will return to a fair value, this Mr. Hatchett hopes and expects. The seasons cannot continue to be as unfavourable as they have been for the last three years without compensating the farmers by higher prices. Those who were able to keep the wheat of last year have obtained a very good price for it. At present the markets are driven down by the large quantity of corn, but I think they will recover as the crops are partially deficient and will not all be well housed. They are in general remarkably good on limestone soils, and I hope they are so on the Spettisbury chalk.

It appears to me the price obtained by Mr. Paxton for Henbury[160] is a very good one and shows that in Dorsetshire it is easier to sell than to let land. Here it is much easier to let than to sell; farmers are here more numerous and more industrious, indeed farming is considered the best trade in these times of general difficulty.

I have one rich neighbour Col. Noel[161] whose health is precarious and his brother, who is his heir, is at present making purchases of land which he will probably do more extensively when like Mr. Drax he comes into the possession of upwards of ten thousand pounds per annum; he may then be very desirous of adding Tunman Wood to those which join it and which are the chief ornaments of his brother's estate. I think also and hope Mr. Collect may be able to sell Swinethorpe to a rich neighbour Col. Jarvis, who has come to reside at Doddington Hall[162], a building which requires a larger domain which keeps up the value of the land; where it is only wanted as investment it sells very low, because farmers, even such as Makrell and Clapcott, are anxious to sell rather than to buy.

As it is necessary for me to continue turning over these things in my mind I have given you another page out of the book of lucubrations that you may make your remarks upon it. If we want to put any plan in execution we cannot create the opportunity, we can only prepare ourselves to sieze it promptly when it occurs. Thus it is my opinion that if anything is to be done with regard to the mortgage it should be done promptly, because we are on the eve of great events, and cannot tell how fast

160 Henbury House, Sturminster Marshall, was built in 1715 for the 1st Earl of Strafford (2nd creation) and enlarged in 1770. It was converted into flats in the 1990s.

161 The Hicks (later Noel) family, Earls of Gainsborough, owned land in Gloucestershire, particularly around Chipping Campden from the 17th century. Baptist Hicks built Campden House in the early part of the 17th century, but it was burnt down by the Royalists in 1645. Only the Gatehouse and two Banqueting Houses remain. A descendant of the Noel family still lives in the town.

162 Doddington Hall near Lincoln was built in the late 16th century. It passed by inheritance to Lt. Col George Jarvis in 1829.

they may come upon us. It is not worth while to wait for the chance of a rise of one per cent in the funds, when there is greater chance of a fall of fifteen or twenty per cent as we experienced five years ago, soon after the funds had reached 94, when from slighter causes that are now in operation they fell nearly down to 70.

The chief question for my own consideration is whether I shall let my land immediately or keep it in hand until I can sell, or let it at a higher rent; but as the events which would facilitate the latter plan would perhaps be as much against the value of funded property; the chance is not worth risking, if it is desirable we should all keep together under one roof; otherwise I should be content to stay here and look after my property; the task is not unamusing to the youngest of our trio, but neither that nor our suitability here compensates for the regret of depriving you of the society of Dorothea and her of yours. The thought of granpa and granma occur no less frequently to Thomasine.

[The letter continues in Dorothea's handwriting. Ed.] The meaning of all which in plain English is, that while we are obliged to pay the exorbitant interest we do upon the mortgage, and we are liable to have that raised, we cannot afford to let the farms for less than we have been accustomed to do, and therefore until a respectable tenant can be procured at that rent we must look after them ourselves; but when the half or better still the whole of the mortgage is paid off, then we could afford to let the land at a lower rate and return to you. We, and I in particular, am therefore most anxious that as far as regards the six thousand pounds at least, this should be done as soon as possible. This was written before we had received yours in which you mention the probable rise of the funds.

I am disposed to rely on Mr. Solly's judgement and with respect to them, but people in London may have better information. Mr. Solly is anxious this letter should go today. I therefore do not wait to know whether the parcel is arrived, but will write again when it does and tell you all about Thomasine who is quite well and happy. Mrs. Harnage has been spending a week with us, she is just the kind of person you would like. I hope Papa continues to take pains about the recovery of his hand, I shall not be happy until it is quite come round again.
In haste your ever affectionate D.S., S.S. & T.J.L.S.
[written on flap of envelope: Lincoln Aug 27.]

D-RAC/E/113. Letter from Mr. S. Solly & Dorothea Solly to the Rev. Thomas and Mrs. Rackett.

Morton, Aug. 12th (1830?)
Dear Papa Mama,
We owe you our thanks for attempting to negotiate a surrender of the mortgage and hope it will not be protracted much longer as the public funds are in a very precarious state, they have recovered for the present through the exertions of Rothschild[163] but

163 Jewish banking family originally from Frankfurt who funded the British war effort in the

if he can work himself out of the scrape they will go down headlong. As he enabled our government to reduce the four per cents by driving up the English funds, he will continue to obtain all the support that can be granted him on this side of the water.

Mr. Herries[164] is supposed to be connected with him privately and has certainly acquired a large property under his guidance. Rothschild contracted for the last French loan and it is the interest of these men who are now at the head of affairs in Paris to support him because the price of the funds is a proof of public confidence. Lafitte and Cassimer Perrier whose names are continually mentioned are bankers and stock jobbers and heads of the commercial interest, they are also protestants. M. Ourrard[165] a great contractor under Bonaparte as well as under the late government has been speculating largely on a fall of the stocks here as well as at Paris and was very successful during the first alarm. He and others who speculate on a fall of stocks will endeavour to renew the alarm but the new government will use their utmost exertions to supress all disturbances at home and prevent all disagreement with foreign countries. If they succeed France will be very nearly assimilated to England, the influence of commercial wealth will predominate in both countries. But will the Holy Alliance allow France to remain in peace, is not the change of dynasty a violation of their fundamental principle. The countries which became united to her during the Revolutionary wars, particularly the Netherlands and Lombardes will invite her to take possession of them again, the former from prediliction, the latter for the sake of securing their own independence. A commotion will certainly take place in Italy and will involve France in a war with Austria, in spite of all the moderation of the constitutional party.

In spite of any temporary calm, the prospect is very much against property in the funds, which would be reduced in value one fourth by a general war, the same cause would raise the value of land and keep up rents but they would also raise the rate of interest to five per cent or higher if the laws against usury are abolished.

These are matters to reflect upon seriously while there is an opportunity of turning to advantage the change of times which otherwise threatens us with loss on both sides.

We wish to get way from hence as soon as possible and meet you in Dorsetshire but Mr. Godsell is not the best of bailiffs and this is a bad time for letting land. Hatchett who boasts of his moderate rents and has made an abatement of fifteen per cent has been obliged to accept Green as a tenant and finds it difficult to get any rent, his soil is a cold clay which whether in grass or in tillage is equally unproductive in these times and seasons, the grass will not fatten cattle it will only rear them and this does not answer at present because the markets are overstocked with lean cattle from Ireland, the three wet seasons have also been very unfavourable to the corn crops on cold clay. Hatchett has therefore reason enough to be out of humour with land. This year the crops are very good on dry soils and I hope you will find the yeild of the

Napoleonic Wars.

164 John Charles Herries (1778-1855), President of the Board of Trade.

165 Gabriel-Julien Ouvrard (1770-1846) was a French financier who played a large role in the economic recovery of France after the fall of the Empire. After enjoying great prestige he became bankrupt, was imprisoned on corruption charges, and died in London.

tythes at Spettisbury by no means deficient. If Obourn intended to remain it would be advantageous to him to renew Mr. Smith's agreement.

I have the satisfaction of saying my own land is chiefly of that kind which is most in request at present the only question is whether I shall let it now or wait the chance of next year. I have an application from the Balfours who are the best farmers on this side of the Humber, they are as their name betokens North Britons. The younger, Andrew, just introduced Scotch husbandry in this neighbourhood and has been very successful. He persuaded his brother David to quit a profession for which he had received a higher education, but the farm he took of Mr. Neville at Thorney has not remunerated him for the great expence he has been at in improving it, and he says the rent is the least part of the expence to a good farmer, he would be a most desirable tenant in every respect and I could depend on having my rent paid as punctually as the dividends, as his brother would be his guarantee. This is more desirable than having a tenant like Green at higher rent.

[The next part of the letter is in Mrs. Solly's writing. Ed]
Mr. Solly has written so much and I am so busy that I only have time and space to add that we are all well, that Thomasine improves in every respect, that we have taken her this afternoon to see the Waylands who were all delighted with her, and have asked us to bring her again on Saturday as two of the children were out. We called also at Sir Edwards who was much pleased with her.

I have just unpacked the looking glasses which were both safe and the greatest luxury we have. We gave several broad or rather downright hints for the Piano Forte but it would not do, they are so silly as to regard it as a piece of furniture. If you could give up your guitar, mandolin or anything I should be very glad of it for the children's sake. We talk of you every day and I wish you were all here. I have had no time for gardening and the weather has been very wet. We thank you for the newspapers which are very interesting at present. We have heard nothing of our nephew whom we expected tho' we have written to Hollis Anthony[166], perhaps if you go near John Street Bedford Row 26, you would be so good as to enquire where Edward Anthony is. We have heard nothing of Miss Solly or anyone else. You do not mention Miss Davies.
Your ever affectionate children
DS., SS. & T.J.L.S.
[Written on flap of envelope by Mr. Solly) The Duke of Bordeaux is heir to the claims of the Stuarts. M.E. Anthony arrived just before we set out this morning by the Englishman. I perceive the King of Naples is dead.

D-RAC/E/102. Letter from Charles Hatchett to Mrs. Rackett.

Belle Vue House, Chelsea
July 18, 1831

166 John Hollis Anthony was practicing as a barrister at 45 Great Ormond Street in 1833.

My Dear Mrs. Rackett,
I must begin this letter with matters of finance and have therefore to acquaint you that on Saturday last I went to the bank and received your Dividend as follows

Dividend due in April)	
on 600 3&½ per Cents)	£10.10.0
Dividend due this July)	
on 12925 3 per Cent Consols)	193.17.6
Do. on 1800 Do.	17. 0.0.
	£231.7.6. [*sic*]

Be so good as to say what you wish to be done with the above stated sum.

And now my Dear Mr. and Mrs. Rackett give me leave to thank you for your letter which I received some time ago and which brought to me such a good account of both of you, and as to that part signed T.R. I had full proof by the fine and full hand in which it was written. Although we regret not to have seen you here, yet I must say that considering the Season I was much surprised that you remained in the Country and by so doing you have perhaps escaped the almost universal disease called Influenza which has been so prevalent that (as an Eminent Physician observed to me) if it had been as fatal as it has been extensive it would be to all extents and purposes a Plague. Some croaking persons will have it is the forerunner of the *Cholera Morbus*, but this is an absurd supposition; I am sorry however to hear from good authority that the real *cholera Morbus* has appeared in Glasgow, although only two cases have as yet been reported, and from prudential motives as little is said as possible about this horrible disease which seems destined to be the Scourge of the World.

But to speak on more cheerful subjects I must tell you that I have seen and heard Paganini and must confess that I was equally surprised and delighted with his most extraordinary performance. Last Thursday I went to the Opera and was enchanted with Past a and Taglione[167]. I would recommend you or your Book Society to get Mr. Crokers Edition of Boswells Life of Dr. Johnson. It is rather bulky, being five large Octavo Volumes, but it contains considerable and valuable additions to former Editions.

We hope to set out about the middle of next month on a Tour of the Suffolk and Norfolk Coast, which we have as yet not visited. Our intention is to stay longest at those places which we shall find most interesting, and probably we shall not return home until the end of October. We hope Mr. & Mrs. Solly and little Thomasine are well, and with our kindest regards to all of you, believe me, My dear Mr. and Mrs. Rackett, Always most truly yours,
Charles Hatchett

167 Marie Taglioni (1804–1884) was a celebrated Swedish/Italian ballet dancer, whose father created the original *La Sylphide* in 1832 at the Paris Opéra as a showcase for her talents.

D-RAC/E/108. Letter from Horace Davis to Mrs. Rackett.

Bath. March 12th 1831
My very dear Aunt,
As I find my Dear Mother has not said one word about the carriage I presume she has left it in particular to me and I think I cannot do better than copy part of the essentials written by Mrs. Knipe to my Mother at the time of her leaving here. As for the time it would take to build one we can be no judges as fortunately Halsted had built a new body on speculation and as my Mother had that very one it was very soon finished. With regard to the dimensions I apprehend if you had one built on purpose you can have it of what size you please but this is easily enquired of the Coachmaker. My Mother's carriage has a Rumble behind but no dickey in front but there is a boot by my Mother preferring to drive en Postilion and not to have her view intercepted by the Driver.

> "Halsteds price is 190£ for which he will furnish a very handsome fashionable Chariot built with the best materials painted varnished lined and trimmed in the most elegant style in any colour you choose, folding Venetian blinds and silk Blinds. The Squabs of the best Morocco leather or silk to your fancy trimmed with worsted lace.
> "The said 190£ includes only the Chariot and the chaise seat all the boxes and accommodations must be paid for in addition.
> "The price of a Handsome Chariot built of the best materials & finished in the best style – 190£
> "The prices are annexed of the following additions.
> X "A Wainscot Trunk to front Boot with locks & keys
> 2-18-0
> X "Drop to driving seat locks &c. &c.
> 1-10-0
> X "Cap box to fit front Panel to the dashing leather fixed with staples, straps, &c. 6-6-0
> Imperial fixed with staples to the roof 7-7-0
> Private locks to the doors & bolts to the Venetian Blinds 1-18-0
> "Handles to the Body

This was torn and we could not find the price but it was under 2£ & my Mother had hers made at Bath forgetting to order them from Halsted and they charged her 2£ for them. They are what we call accommodation handles which you take hold of to get into the carriage and I thought it odd that neither these nor a drag chain or Pole were found. My Mother had the additions marked with crosses but I am not sure you would like the last viz. the Cap box, & if strictly kept for very light things I think it an excellent thing tho some are very partial to it. It fixes upon the front panel and I by no means think it advisable to have heavy things put into it for it is an awkward thing in that case to put into its place and unless people are as clever as you and I they might scratch the panel. I will try to give you a sketch of its situation I have marked it with an o and it is under the front glasses it is made of leather like an Imperial.

I have now parted from Mrs. Knipes letter the Paragraphs marked which are all that are essential and I will now say that my Mothers chariot is universally admired and certainly very handsome of course you may choose your own lace furniture &c. – and I must say we considered it very reasonable it is extremely well built. I have now left but little room to say it is quite delightful to see how well & happy my dearest Mother is & she enjoys her little parties of 4 to Quadrille Whist & Cribbage.

D-RAC/E/107. John Knowles to Revd. Thomas Rackett

Revd. Dear Sir,
The late measure of Government, which was in itself as bold as any out of Poligniacs[168] has set the whole country in a ferment, and as such I presume you are not free from its influence. My friend a Mr. Francis Knowles is at Shaftesbury, and he tells me (what I doubt) pretty certain of success. And if he be successful I do not see to what it will lead. Great devastation was made in the windows in the town the night before the last. I did not illuminate and strange to say did not suffer. All the club houses had their windows broken, this clearly proves to me, what the " sovereignty of the people" will end in, it is but the first letter in the Radical Reformer's alphabet.

Although I have been of liberal principles all my life time, yet I dread the results of "the Bill". I am daily in expectation of the arrival of Dr. Temple in England, he comes to pay a visit to me and will remain a month or six weeks, the Doctor brings with him, all the correspondence from Fuseli to Lavater from the year 1763 to 1779, this a year or two since would have been invaluable to me; he found then, where he little expected, in the possession of Lavater's youngest daughter. I shall however embrace this information for a second edition of my work. Mr. Roscoe has written me a very flattering letter commending highly my life of Fuseli for its "truth and characteristic merits", and regretting that his great age and infirmities prevented him from giving me assistance there in. The work has had a good sale, particularly so for the times, for literature and everything else of late is sunk in politics. Although there was an election last night for three persons to be of the Council of the Royal Society, there was a lamentable show of empty benches. Mr. Thomas Solly is in better health, he is now enabled occasionally to leave his house. Captain Vincent has got the cross of the Guelphic order, it was sent him yesterday by the King and he was told that no fees are to be paid. Coburn & Co. bring out on Monday the life of Sir Thomas Lawrence. I am told by a competent judge (Dr. Paris) who has seen the work that "it is dull stuff". I beg my kindest respects to Mrs. Rackett
And am, Revd. Dear Sir,

168 A.J.A.M. Polignac, Prince de, 1780-1847. (HSLD) Count Jules de Polignac French statesman and ultra-royalist who served as Prime Minister under Charles X and escaped France after the July revolution in 1830.

Your faithful and devoted
John Knowles.
Navy Office
29 April 1831.

D-RAC/E/113. Letter from Dorothea Solly to Rev. T. & Mrs. Rackett & Thomasine.

Bracken Cottage
Oct. 1st & 2nd
(1832)
Dear Papa & Mama &, Sweet little girl.
I think I told you that Dr. Warwick[169] was to give a lecture at the Half way House to accommodate Sir Edward, ourselves & the Waylands & that he & his son spent Saturday and Sunday with us last week. We performed some glees & duets composed by Dr. Warwick's daughter, Mrs. Thompson, which were very good, and also all the Italian duets that I happen to have here, which are not many, but some of Paers[170] very beautiful, from the opera of *Leonora*, we have also contrived to get through, so as to hear the effect of the exquisite *canone* in Beethoven's *Fidelio* which is published in the Harmonicon for August. As Sir Edward and ourselves had guarranteed the profit of 15 persons at 3/- a ticket we made it known to the neighbourhood and though many people that promised did not come yet we took upwards of 4 pounds, and had attendance of about 30 people. The meeting was held at Glaziers as being the largest room and was honoured by the attendance of Sir Ed. Broomhead[171], Col. & Mrs. Jarvis of Doddington Hall, Mr. & Mrs. Lister, Mr. & Mrs. & Miss Wayland, Mr. Bogue, Miss Naylor, some farmers, some of our own tenants whom we treated, &c. &c. A variety of interesting and brilliant experiments were shewn, as the formation of water, the ascent of a baloon, the spontaneous inflammation of Phosphoretted Hydrogen gas with its beautiful rings of smoke &c. but the novelties to us were amperes rotations[172], shewing the revolution of the magnetic round the influence, of the galvanic wire on the magnetic needle in turning it out of

169 Dr Thomas Olivers Warwick (1772-1852) born in Nottingham. He trained at a Dissenting Academy well-known for providing its students with lectures on scientific matters, becoming minister of the Presbyterian chapel at Rotherham. He began to deliver public lectures on scientific subjects, in London in 1798, and subsequently in Sheffield, Manchester and elsewhere. In 1805 he was partner (probably with his father-in-law) in a manufactory at Rotherham making chemicals for fixing dye colours; the partnership was declared bankrupt in 1816.

170 Paer, Fernando (1771-1839), Italian Musical Composer. His opera *Leonora* (1804) is stated to have the same base as Beethoven's *Fidelio.* (HSLD)

171 Sir Edward Broomhead, 2nd Baronet, (1789-1855) of Thurlby Hall, Kesteven. Whilst at Cambridge, he was founder of the Analytical Society with Charles Babbage, John Herschel and George Peacock. He was President of the Lincoln Mechanics Institute, where he met the young George Boole and supplied him with mathematical books to encourage his studies.

172 Ampere is the basic unit of electrical current, named after the French scientist André Marie Ampère (1775-1836).

its course, the formation of a magnet of immense power by connecting it with plates of zinc in andacid of a foot diameter – The magnet capable of supporting 200lb. weight while in connexion with the battery. Last of all he shewed the brilliant light produced by a stream of oxygen & Hydrogen on a globule of red hot lime.

He threw out some speculation on the possibility of the motion of the earth round its axis as being caused by the magnetic & galvanic forces, and also of their influence on the laws of animal life, and mentioned the Galvanoscope which shews by means of a very fine magnetic needle the effect of the mere contraction of the nerve of an animal in turning it out of its course.

Everybody of course was highly gratified; we had Miss Naylor, who is musical and had no other means of coming, to spend a day or two with us; and she was quite delighted with her visit. The Waylands dined with us after the lecture and Mr. Bogue who is with them & returned in the evening; very much pleased with Dr. Warwick who is a very pleasant man.

It is to him we owe the brilliant yellows that have delighted our eyes in the Linen drapers shops, he also invented a permanent green, dyed in one operation for furniture prints. He had an establishment for the process near Manchester, but a man in his employ broke in through a hole in the roof of his work room, discovered the secret, and deprived him of the whole profit of his invention. Of course we have had much conversation on the art of Dyeing in which I used to take so much interest & I shall try his processes when I have an opportunity. The yellow is dyed with chrome: the cotton is boiled in a subacetate of lead or Goulards Extract[173] which becomes intimately united with the fibre of the cotton, and then in Chromate of Potash. The yellow is quite permanent. If it is then dipped in boiling lime water it becomes a brilliant orange. The green is produced by alumina being dissolved in the Alkaline solution of Muriate of Ammonia; the Muriatic Acid combines with the potash, leaving the Alumina[174] in the cloth which would otherwise be dissolved again in the hot water and cause the colour to run when plunged in the yellow dye of Quercitron Bark[175]. Of course you will not mention these secrets to any one likely to make use of them as they are not yet generally known.

We received your kind letter and are very glad to hear of your all being well and of our darlings riding upon the donkey which will do her good. We always wish to be remembered to our friends in Dorsetshire; you say Mr. Cooke is coming into the North, pray give our kind regards to him & say we would be happy to see him in his way. I draw up a few strings of my Piano Forte occasionally so as to be able to make it tolerable, and we have borrowed a flute for Mr. Warwick who remains for a few days to shoot while his father prepares the way at Grantham where he is to lecture on Friday. It is quite a treat for me to perform some duets of Paer and Cimarosa[176] which I never had the opportunity of trying before. We are invited to dine to day at Mrs. Naylors to

173 Goulard's Extract = Liq. plumbi Subacet. fort. (HSLD)
174 Alumina = Alumina Oxide (HSLD)
175 Quercitron Bark = Bark of *Quercus tinctoria* (HSLD)
176 Domenico Cimarosa (1749-1801), Italian composer of light operas.

meet her brother Major Stretton who is just come from abroad.

We are very glad the dear child has some children to play with now and then; we have two very amusing kittens tell her, one yellow and one like Smut. My China Aster is in great request, Mrs. Lister has some beauties from it, but those I have from being choked with weeds before I came down are very stunted and very small tho' very double and would make a pretty garland for my sweet Thomasine. All we wish is that you were with us, I am sure you would enjoy our music. We cannot boast of your deserts, but we have had some peaches, and one of our tenants has his house literally covered with grapes from a vine which I gave him. Our own have some, tho' under the projecting roof. Mr. Solly wishes you to keep the Bank Charter papers till they are completed. He knows of no relations in the West. They are probably of the Worcestershire Sollys, to whom as yet he has not been able to trace relationship. Have you found any more coins?

We had brought in yesterday 4½ brace of partridges 2 hares one rabbit & one pheasant, but Mr. Warwick would have done better by himself, for Mr. Bogues dog behaved ill and his gun would not go off. We have plenty of game they say of all kinds; do you think Horace Davis would be induced to pay us a visit; we intended to write to him but have had so much to do. I must now conclude as Mr. Solly takes this to Lincoln with Mr. Warwick who after a walk of 20 miles or more will join us at tea with Mrs. Naylors, he has been out shooting since six o'clock.
Your affectionate & dutiful D.S. S.S.

D-RAC/E/113. Letter from Dorothea & Samuel Solly to Rev. Th. & Mrs. Rackett, addressed to Gower Street.

Coulsterworth, Wednesday (1832)
Dear Papa & Mama,
Tho we have not got on quite so far as we had expected owing to the bad weather on Sunday, yet we have had a very prosperous journey without rain, and the little thing has really enjoyed herself. We set off from Forty Hall at about half past nine on Monday and got to Royston at 7 o'clock, the little dear having slept almost all the way from Ware where she had some dinner. We saw a card there at a Museum of Roman Antiquities lately discovered consisting of Urns, Tesselated Pavements, stoves for the baths, &c. &c., but after we had had our tea we found it would be too dark to see the things but hope to go another time. We got away at ½ past eight next morning and got to Godmanchester, a distance of 20 miles without stopping, the little girl having slept most part of the way and was very lively when awake. There we all had mutton chops and our 13 mile stage afterwards, to Norman Cross was enlivened by Miss Thomasine who laughed and talked the whole way. So she did this morning and after dinner slept for above two hours, the whole of the last stage.

We had intended making our long halt at Stamford, and got there ½ past eleven, but as we came near the town, symptoms appeared of the proximity of the Races, and on enquiry found they were to commence this afternoon. We therefore merely stopped for a minute at the Cooksons who were much pleased to see the child, and drove on to Casterton 3 miles farther, where we took some veal and ham that were just ready for the family and there being a Piano, some music, a cat and a nice garden we remained there some hours and then came on here, our favourite sleeping place, as it was impossible to get to Newark today.

Newark. Thursday.
You may now congratulate us on having happily arrived at the end of our journey as we shall stay here to night, Mr. Solly having to speak to his man of business. We made but one stage from Coulsterworth here a distance of 21 miles and Bunby, who often goes best at the end of a journey, went much faster than he had done before. We got here at one o'clock, the child enjoying herself all the way by the help of the story of Poor Dick, and the songs of I've been at Kensington, and the Dog upon 4 legs, &c. she is now at dinner with Harriet on some lamb which was prepared for the stage coach. Both my boxes are arrived and I shall open them presently. The beautiful geranium *pratense* grows in profusion between this and Stamford. The Election Flags are already hung out here, at Stamford and Huntingdon[177].

The little dear is very well and merry and sends her love and a kiss to you both. We often talk about you, and hope you take care of yourselves. The rain on Sunday did not extend as far as Buckden. Mr. Solly is going to drive to Norton and return here as his man of business will not be home till evening. As soon as we have made ourselves tidy I shall take Missy to call on Mrs. Lacey &c.
Your ever dutiful & affectionate,
D.S. S.S. F.T.L.S.

D-RAC/E/107. John Knowles to Rev. Thomas Rackett.

Revd. Dear Sir,
We may ask a banker or a merchant for a Sunday frank, and the more so, I think if it be directed to one of his customers, so I put this under a cover of my friend Biddulph. At any rate it will give to your collection the hand writing of a Reformer in <u>this</u> Reformed <u>Parliament</u>. Received on Thursday last your dividends £153, and on my return wrote to Mr. Lister to receive £69.0.6. on Mr. Solly's account this is, £75 minus £5.19.6. paid for the Parliamentary taxes which you desired me to deduct. Mr. Lister not having yet paid me a visit the account stands thus

(Cocks & Co. rects.	£78.0.0
(Mr. Solly's taxes	5.19.6.
(Received for Mr. Solly)	<u>69.0.6.</u>
(to be paid Mr. Lister)	£153.0.0

177 Parliament was dissolved on 3rd December 1832 and a General Election was called. Politically, it was a turbulent year, with the passing of the Reform Bill in June.

Since my last I have paid the parochial taxes and the impost for lighting cleaning &c. which we can talk about when we meet.

The first measure of the new Parliament on a grand scale, will it is said, be a reform of the Church, it will be well if they do not undermine the ancient fabric, for if you destroy an establishment of this kind you will create what is most dreaded to be, general irreligion. The Government has certainly a right to do what they think proper, for the future, with regard to those who may accept livings under this immediate gift, because there is a compact between the giver and the receiver; but more than half this property is in the hands of laymen, who in this respect have the oldest and best right to property in this Kingdom, for in all times this right has been respected. These notions may not be new but I have seen them nowhere. Perhaps I may tell you news, when I say the views of the Reformers are to have only two Archbishops and two Bishops for England, the stalls to be retained, but to be given to the poorest livings under the Crown. Every establishment requires to [be] upheld by dignity and importance and I will ask whether this is the way to keep them up?

What is called the civil society in which we now live, is composed of Knaves and quacks who know nothing and esteem no one who knows anything. This is not the language of a disappointed man, for I am highly satisfied with one measure (a selfish idea you will say) if that measure be confirmed by a Reformed and reforming Parliament, but it arises now from the reflections of a cool minded spectator who sees nothing but barrenness.

On the Navy I could say much, but God deliver me from having anything more to do with it. This great arm of strength is however in a rapid decline. To pass to more pleasant subjects I have seen the Suffolk Street Gallery[178], composed of the work of the living and dead artists of England, the latter however predominating. It is a poor assemblage of talent on walls of a great extent, and some of the worst specimens of artists. I speak of those which are genuine take my word for it, there are many copies. For instance of three pictures of Fuseli which are exhibited two are known copies.

The Royal Society is well attended, the Duke however of late has been absent from indisposition and interdicted by Dr. Maton from leaving the house. The Doctor appears to change but little, except in teeth, pitty it is he does not consult our friend Cartwright[179], who could in this particular furnish "stock in trade". There are many men whose voice and appearance are not injured by loss of teeth – not so with Dr. Maton.

I am expecting hourly to see Sir Rt. Seppings[180] who is coming to stay a few weeks with me, the absence of employment bears heavily upon him, perhaps it would upon me if I had not now employment. The human mind appears to want direction by compulsion – I speak now only of men who have been engaged during the best

178 Home to the Society of British Artists, founded in 1823. Their first exhibition was held in 1824. The Society acquired a royal charter in 1887 and now exhibits at the Mall Galleries.
179 Samuel Cartwright, who had a dental practice at 32 Old Burlington Street.
180 Sir Robert Seppings (1767-1840), naval Architect, was inventor of 'Sepping's Blocks' for suspending vessels in docks. Surveyor of the Navy, 1813-32. F.R.S. 1814. (HSLD)

period of life in active avocations.

You ask me for the subject of the seal which closes the envelope, it is I believe Hercules with "the Nemean lions skin", you know the ancients terminated their figures of giants with serpents' tails. I am open to a better explanation.

Everything here goes on to my satisfaction, some alterations have been made which everyone must allow are improvements, but I believe even under a change of systems, everyone esteems me.

I beg my respectful compliments to Mrs. Rackett and kind remembrance to Thomasine and believe me My Dear Sir to be
Your affectionate friend
and devoted Servant
John Knowles
20 Jany. 1833.

D-RAC/E/113. Letter from Dorothea and Samuel Solly to Rev. T. & Mrs. Rackett.

Bracken Cottage. Feb. 4th 1833
Dear Papa & Mama & sweet innocent Lambkin,
We had no room to say in our last how much we were delighted to receive your letter particularly as it came after a disappointment. Mr. Solly having enquired at Lincoln and found none there but brought this from the Half way House. We are glad to find our dear little Girl is a favourite with everybody and we are much obliged to Mrs. White and all her other friends for their goodness to her. We wish we could see you my pretty darling sitting on Grandpapa's knee and reading with him. Pray give our love to Mrs. White and all our friends.

We have been out all the week – on Monday to the Listers where supposing it to be a family party I went in my morning dress, but we found there Capt. & Mrs. Barth very nice people whom we had not met there before and as the next day was very wet we spent till Wednesday. I shewed Mrs. Lister how to join netting for one of the long Boa tippets in Lambs wool in imitation of those made of feathers, and trimmed her a turban which looks very well. On Wednesday morning we drove first home to change our packages and clothes and then to Burton 3 miles beyond Lincoln. Luckily they did not dine till 6 o'clock or we should have been late; it was rather a formal dinner as the Precentor Mr. Pretyman and his lady dined there for the first time, the Dean had been asked but declined on account of King Charles's Martyrdom[181], so did another family in Lincoln.

Mr. Fardell of Lincoln was there and two officers one of whom knows the Monro's as his father has the appointment at the Cape and he said Mrs. Monro had been very kind to his sisters. His name is Bird, they were both pleasant men. The next day being a hard frost we walked in to Lincoln with Mr. Whitehead who wanted the Charlesworths to meet us but they could not. I called on Mrs. Havenega who

181 Charles I was executed on 30th January 1649 and is commemorated on that day.

walked down the town with me. She desired me to ask where these Lamberts live that you mention, as she thinks she knows something of them. We returned to Mr. Whiteheads to dinner and in the evening had music, Mrs. Whitehead plays very well has a charming Grand Piano of Broadwood's and a very large collection of music, Mr. Whitehead sings a little; they have Clarke's Handel[182] which I enjoyed much.

As that was our wedding day which we did not recollect when we made the engagement we asked the Listers & Dr. Morton to dine the next day with us, so we were obliged to come home through the snow which had fallen in the night but it soon began to melt and was not slippery. We had a snug sociable day and a pool at Quadrille and drunk all your healths. The real wedding day was kept by our servant Collisham and the tenants wives in Lincolnshire stile [sic] with tea and hot cakes. Susan, Mrs. Linney and Harriet's sister were of the party her mother being afraid to venture at his time of year, but she desired me to give her love to Harriet and to say she was pretty well. Mrs. Harnage and her sister enquire much after you all and desired their kind regards.

I forgot to mention in my last that Lady Lincoln was at one of the Newark balls and charmed everybody by her beauty, affability and Scotch dancing. Shall we send you some of our potatoes for seed? And how many? I should like of all things to speculate upon Mr. O'Kelly's property if we could get rid of this, what cottages I would build and what gardens I would lay out, and all so close to you it would be delightful. Dr. Morley has lent me two Vols. of the Harmonicon music like those of Mrs. Brandes. I wish you would get that for last August (I think Miss Smith of the Down House[183] has it with the account of Miss Davies the songs the Armonica &c. put in by Mr. Parry.)

[The letter continues in Samuel Solly's writng. Ed.]
Many persons imagine the poor rates may be nearly done away by letting plots of ground to the poor for cultivation of potatoes, this would raise the value of land as it has done in Ireland, where the distress does not arise from the sub-letting system and over population but from indolence and turbulence occasioned by the want of Education to which the Catholic priesthood are generally hostile. Sir Bernard observed to the Bishop of Durham in recommendation of the schools established by the latter, that after the reformation as a check to the pauperism it occasioned, the Scotch established schools while we enacted poor laws which have demoralised the poor by making them improvident. The savings banks may prove a check to this evil but hitherto the depositors have been mostly inhabitants of the towns where they are established; the village labourers ought to be encouraged to deposit the surplus of their weekly wages which while they are single often amount to one half if they are fully employed. The married men here say they cannot maintain their families with less than two shillings a day – if they cannot earn that they demand it of the parish but the single men can subsist on 8d. a day. An Irishman can subsist on 2d. a day in idleness. It is the [an

182 John Clarke (later Clarke-Whitfield) (1770-1836) was an organist and composer, and a pioneer in editing Handel's oratorios. He was Professor of Music (Cambridge) from 1821 until his death.

183 The Down House near Blandford was the seat of Sir John Smith

illegible word here. Ed.] of subsistence, the consequent temptation to idleness that is the principal course of distress not only in Ireland but in this country through the working of the poor laws. The complaints are general here of the lapses of farms from bad seasons but those who have given up their farms in hopes of gaining by exchange begin to find themselves like players at commerce obliged to be contented with worse that they have parted with. The competition for moderate sised [sic] farms never was greater than at present, the spirit of improvement instead of being checked is rather excited by the failure of the crops but increases the preference given for dry soils. The strong clays formerly acclaimed the best wheat land are getting more and more behind hand but while in some places they are allowed of cultivation, in Hatchetts property & many others the tenants are allowed to break up more grass land because the sheep have been destroyed by the rot, cattle are unprofitable.

Have you tried the Oblique Pens they seem very nice things. We have been recommended to read *Recollections of my Life* by Taylor[184] of the Opera House. Kiss our dear for us both, and believe us your dutiful & affectionate D.S.S.S.

We have read Campbells memoirs with much pleasure. We have Babbages[185] book now. Some of Miss Martineus[186] tales are good but Mrs. S. does not like her *Political Economy*. We are to have Moriers *Hostage*[187] soon.

D-RAC/E/102. Letter from Charles Hatchett to Rev. Th. Rackett.

Belle Vue House,
Chelsea.
13 Feby. 1833.
Dear Mr. & Mrs. Rackett,
Your letter came to me on Friday last and on the following day Mess. Couts's Bought one Hundred Consols in my name and that of Mr. H. Davis at 87¼

£87.5.0.)
) £87.7.6
Broker 2.6.)
Monday 11th Feby. Paid as requested
to the account of Mr. Rackett at
Cocks and Biddulphs 145.15.0
being the amount of Dividends received £233.2.0

I hope that both of you are now quite well and wish I could say so as to my wife,

184 John Taylor, (1752-1833), *Records of my Life*, 1833.
185 Charles Babbage (1791-1871), *On the Economy of Machinery and Manufactures*, 1832.
186 Harriet Martineau (1802-1876). She published monthly treatises on politicians and economists of the day. Her first book, *Illustrations of Political Economy* was published in 1832.
187 John Morier (1780-1849), Author of *The Adventures of Hajj Baba of Ispahan* (1824), *Zohrab the Hostage* (1832), etc. (HSLD)

but although the fever has been subdued yet she remains in a state of extreme debility, and I fear it will be a long time before she will recover he former health. The lamentable affair concerning Mr. Lambert and Mr. Hannam is much talked of, and the *Morning Herald* of this day states "that the alleged Crim Con[188] in Dorsetshire is taken up throughout the County with so much party zeal, that it has become a matter of consideration whether the Venue in the action about to be tried must not be changed" - is Mr. Hannam, the Brother of him who married Miss Morgan, or is he the same person?

You may easily imagine what a dull time I have had ever since Christmas, and had it not been for my Library I know not what I could have done, for my wife's nerves are so shaken that she cannot bear Music; I have however been somewhat amused by some information communicated to me upon a subject which you will be surprised to learn is Dog stealing. This is now carried on upon a regular and systematic plan in London and its environs. The Chieftain of the Dog stealers resides in the neighbourhood of Kensington in a good House and excepting Dog stealing is said to be a very decent and apparently respectable person. In respect to Dog stealing this man (whose name is Sexton) is the Jonathan Wild[189] of our times, only he never causes any of his associates to be convicted as Jonathan Wild did, but like him he enables those whose dogs have been stolen to recover them again upon their paying a stipulated reward. He has I understand a regular Report and description of all Dogs which are stolen made to him daily, and especially of fancy and sporting Dogs. Two of my friends have lately been obliged to have recourse to him and the amount of the reward being arranged, he named a place and Day when in these two several cases my friends servants were to meet a person to whom the money was to be paid. These persons then conducted the Servants to a house at the back of the Temple and having shown them into a Room took leave of them and in a few minutes the skirting board of the Room was partially opened by a sliding Door like that of a Dog Kennel and in walked the Dog without any body being seen to deliver him. In one case a fortnight having elapsed after the time which had been named for restoring a valuable Dog, the owner applied to Mr. Sexton to know the cause of the delay, when Sexton assured him that eventually he might rely on having his Dog restored to him, but to say the truth, a Gentleman had seen and having fallen in love with the Dog had bought him at a very high price and therefore it was thought as a matter of conscience no more than fair to let him have the pleasure of keeping the Dog for one month before he was again to be stolen to restore him to his old Master. If I had room I could tell you a good deal more upon this very amusing subject. My wife and Mr. and Mrs. Brande send their kindest

188 William Charles Lambert (1797-1857) a barrister of Winterbourne Steepleton and Knowle House (Wimborne) was staying, with his wife Georgiana, at High Hall, Pamphill, the home of W Hannam. Mr. Lambert claimed to have found his wife undressed in Hannam's bedroom. Following an altercation, Hannam considered himself ill-used and sent a challenge to Lambert. There were hearings in the Court of King's Bench, and adultery ('criminal conversation') was found not proved, but there were further scandals involving Lambert's wife over the next two years.

189 Jonathan Wild: English Informer, 1682-1725. (HSLD)

regards, and I am,
My Dear Mr. & Mrs. Rackett
Yours always most Truly,
Chas. Hatchett.

D-RAC/C/70. Letter from John Warton, Oxford[190].

Opposite St. John's Coll.
15th Feby .1833
Dear Sir,
I came here last Novr. in search of a situation as a Translator & Teacher of Persian & am happy to say that I have experienced the greatest attention & kindness from Dr. McBride head of Magdalene Hall ______ a few other Professors have also aided me but I have as yet obtained no fixed or certain means, therefore my situation is next to being destitute _______an opening however has presented itself of which , if I can be enabled to avail myself I should be as well off as I was in Persia in 1816 when I had 600L a year from the Persian Prince _____ The Turkish Ambassador Numick Pacha would take me with his suite to Constantinople where I am to enter the service of the Sultan. _______ I have written on this subject to his excellency and have had an answer to my most perfect satisfaction from the Secretary to the Turkish Embassy.

Having thus premised; I can only add such an advantageous prospect can hardly present itself to me in England, and long distress & want of Employment make me most anxious to seize this opportunity of setting myself up for Life.

Your knowledge of my father and family will I trust prompt you on this occasion to assistance _______ I cannot present myself to the Ambassador in the shabby state of my present attire, but if under any consideration you could kindly advance me the 10L I should not only remember the kindness of such benevolent aid with gratitude, but should feel proud to convince you of the importance of such aid, by remitting you the sum advanced on my arrival in Turkey ____ I trust therefore you will kindly and promptly favour me with a reply to this Application ______ I can never expect another opportunity so favourable as the present _________ Since I have been at Oxford I have been comparatively comfortable – but, previously in London you cannot think how greatly I suffered __________ So in every point of view I must strive to join the Ambassador's Suite, My Brother Joseph and his wife are in Town _________ He always speaks of your kindness to him I can only hope I may not be forgotten on the present occasion ________ I hope Mrs. Rackett and all your Family are quite well & beg to offer my humble wishes that every blessing of the New Year, may be theirs and your happy lot __________I am delighted with the aspect of this Venerable place, but depressed by the proof, that Time has taken away all my dearest Relatives __________ Hoping to

190 It would appear Rackett was often generous in his response to begging letters; G.J. Davies, *Somerset and Dorset Notes and Queries*, Vol. XXXV, Pt. 353, March 2001, Pp. 30-33 describes how Rackett supported John Fitzgerald Pennie, an unsuccessful author from East Lulworth.

hear from you, I remain, with every good wish My dear Sir,
Your Very faithful & Obt. Humble Servant,
John Warton.

D-RAC/C/48. Letter from the Rev. J. Cooke, of Chettle & Blandford to the Rev. T.Rackett.

Blandford May 10th 1833.
My dear Sir,
On the day after the receipt of your letter I called on John Ford and executed your commission with him and found on enquiry that a considerable number of Skeletons were found near the buildings opposite Miss Matthews's – Six altogether side by side as would be the case in a cemetary – the heads towards the South East – a single Skeleton very perfect was discovered at a little distance from the above – There were many detached bones found all supposed to be human and not any mixture of animal bones.

Not far from the foundations recently laid on digging the depth of a common spade several coins were turned up one of them a Greek coin was procured by Ford from the man who sent you a coin with a hole in it – You will know the one I mean – You may purchase it if you think fit – This is the only one we have been able to obtain – Five minutes before I called at Charlton this morning Ford obtained for himself the small British coin just dug up in Answorth's garden – the last house in the Blacksmiths Row at C. leading to the River – Enclosed I forward both – I made Ford point out the exact situation of his Potatoe ground where the Greek and Roman coins were found by himself. They were in a circular space of about Thirty yards in diamr. – He informs me the number exceeded Twenty – Four copies of the same and either three or five copies of another kind – Thus there were a dozen or more all diverse – I carefully examined the ground with him but without any fortunate result – there were no traces of Roman pottery brick or tile.

I have not heard when the Visitation[191] is likely to take place it usually is in June; you will probably see it announced in due time in the Salisbury Journal of which I believe you obtain a sight – We have the Influenza as extremely in Blandford as you have in Town and some cases at Charlton – I have hitherto escaped – Mrs. White has been very ill indeed lately – for the last two days she has considerably improved – having had good rest – her general health is better. The Basket will contain above 400 Asparagus a quarter of Lamb – Three Chicken from Mrs. Crosse and two couple of Pigeons from Foster who begs me to thank you for a very fine Fish – You sent one to Mr. Bastard which I pronounce to have been most excellent – I must not omit thanking you for the German production you were so kind to send me. With kind remembrances to Mrs. Rackett Miss Thomasine & Mr. & Mrs. S. if with you.

191 Both the Bishop and the Archdeacon conducted regular Visitations of their parishes, to check on the spiritual and moral conduct of the churches in their area.

I remain, Very sincerely Yrs.,
J. Cooke.

D-RAC/E/113. Letter from Dorothea and Samuel Solly to Rev. T. & Mrs. Rackett.

Nov. 9th (1833)
Dear Papa & Mama,
We received your nice letter yesterday and were very glad to find Mama was able to write tho' sorry she is not quite well. We had a letter from Mr. Clarke [Cooke – see below] some days ago from London in which he says he shall be here either the end of this week or beginning of next so that we are expecting him; Thomasine has been talking of nothing else ever since, but she thought at first that of course Grandpa & Grandma would come with him. She thinks nothing of an eight mile ride on her Donkey which she has taken frequently with us both to Bassingham and Collingham, she grows fat and firm eats well and relishes everything has cocoa for breakfast with her Papa is very fond of cabbage carrots turnips & onions and as everything agrees with her she eats as we do. She is quite robust and blooming I assure you and is always out in the garden with me and often very useful. She is as good as ever and delights everybody with her pretty ways. She gets on with her music knows her notes on the paper, plays the scale in many different keys knows major from minor and various other things. She is my constant companion in short during the day and a very amusing one.

Tho' we have had not so much game as we ought we have had sufficient for ourselves, Pettinger shoots for us and lately a young man of the name of Spooner who is the son of a clergyman at Scarle. Our little dear can eat the whole breast of a partridge and enjoyed a wood pigeon the other day extremely. It is a very juicy bird like wild duck. We kill a porker next week and have a hare and brace of rabbits in the house so that we shall be well provided for Mr. Cooke. I wish you could taste an apple we have called the Duke of Coblin it is the finest apple for roasting I ever saw so large and juicy but not a keeping apple. We had some fruit for the first time on Papa's pear trees which were very fine. I envy your flowers; the Yuccas must be magnificent. Papa's drawing is very nice indeed. The white frost has struck our garden sooner than our neighbours I suppose because we are not walled round.

Mrs. Kendall has just got a daughter. We are to go to Mrs. Harnages next Friday for a few days. They have established a Mechanics Institute at Lincoln of which Sir Ed. Bromhead is to be President, they talk of branch societies in all the principal towns of this country. We will send you the papers with the speeches as you will see how far Lincolnshire is before Dorset in intellectual Progress. They have already a library Society, a Musical Association and a Mechanics Library besides <u>the</u> Library and yet the tone of Society in the higher ranks there is decidedly and exclusively card playing. It is

Sir Ed. Bromhead and Dr. Charlesworth[192] who take such pains to Intellectualize them and yet are opposed in almost everything. We have been reading *De Foix* a historical Novel by Mr. Bray[193] with good descriptions of the manners of the 14th century. She was the widow of Stodhard[194] the painter.

Sunday.
You will see by the Lincoln paper what the plan of the Mechanics Institute is, we are just come from Sir Edward who tells us that their meeting room is to be an ancient school house[195] about 60 feet long with arched stone roof &c. This is to be warmed by stoves and they are to have a museum in it with a person to take care of it. They are also to have conversaziones and lectures. We had a card from Mr. Cooke to day left as he passed the Half Way House yesterday evening in his way to his aunts at Lincoln to say that he will he here on Tuesday to dinner. We have asked sir Edward to meet him. We have had a remarkably fine season for sowing wheat and we hope the prospect for next year is good. I have had an estimate of the land and wood I have offered to Mr. Neville but the latter is taken only at its value to cut down now. The number of oaks is supposed to be 10,000 which must in 20 years become worth 20,000, therefore I value them at half that sum at present though they would not make more than a fourth of it if they were cut down now. I have agreed to accept £8000 for the wood but do not like to part with it for £6000 or £6500 which is the price talked of, young oak wood being worth only a shilling per cubic foot. This fall in price to less than one half makes the wood barely worth what it was valued at eighteen years ago instead of having doubled in value as it ought to have done but other kinds of property particularly houses have fared worse. Oak timber must become dearer than ever in case of another war but of this the danger seems to be daily lessening through the influence of the liberal policy which is strengthening itself throughout the west of Europe. These schemes of Russia have been most fortunately marr'd by De Ponza[196].
We are ever your very dutiful & affectionate with many kisses from Thomasine who desires her love to Mrs. White and all friends.
S.S. D.S. T.S.

D-RAC/C/70. Letter to Rev. T. Rackett from R.C.C. Pooley, Blandford, appealing for

192 Dr.Edward Parker Charlesworth (1783-1853), physician to Lincoln County Hospital and pioneer of mental health treatment.

193 Anna Eliza Bray (1790-1883), author of many books. *De Foix, a Romance of Bearn* was published in 1826.

194 John Stothard (1755-1824). Anne Eliza Bray, the author, was first married to Charles Stothard, son of the painter, antiquarian and draughtsman with a particular interest in monumental effigies. He died in 1821.

195 The Mechanics Institute in Lincoln met in the Greyfriars, the surviving portion of the former Friary. After the Dissolution it was used as a school. It is now used for temporary exhibitions.

196 'Carlos de Ponza' was the alias used by Admiral Sir Charles Napier (1786-1860) in the Napoleonic Wars.

a subscription for a local Artist, probably Alfred Stevens. Dated 10 Jany. 1834.

Sir,
I trust you will pardon the liberty I am now taking in forwarding the enclosed list to you. The fact is young Stevens[197], our native self-taught (or rather inate artist) of whose abilities I believe you have seen some specimens, has received a most liberal and handsome offer from a Gentleman of this neighbourhood, now in Italy, for him to be sent immediately to him at Florence, and that he will be at the expence of his studies whilst there; - Such a splendid offer cannot of course be rejected by his parents, and, as I also know, his friends are not in circumstances to do much more than clothe him, for his voyages; I have a wish to place a small sum of money in his pocket, when he leaves ___ Should my object meet with your approbation, any little sum you might think proper to contribute will be thankfully received, but should the step I have taken not meet with your approval I trust you will lay the blame on my shoulders, as his friends are quite unconscious of the steps I am taking, and, perhaps would dissapprove, were they aware of them. I beg to say that I do not intend to extend this application, but to a very few gentlemen who have known the boy. I remain Sir, with the greatest respect,
Your most obt. R.C.C. Pooley.

D-RAC/E/102. Letter from Charles Hatchett to Mrs. Rackett.

Belle Vue House,
Chelsea,
21 January, 1834
My dear Mrs. Rackett,
I must begin by asking what I am to do with your Dividends which I have received; the amount is the same as in the last account of July namely £234.12.6. And now Domine Rackett let me have a little talk with you about your Breeches Bible, and whilst I am ready to admit with you that the female Descendants of Eve have discovered a Universal propensity to wear clothes, yet I am convinced that Eve did not wear them and that the word Breeches introduced in that Edition of the Bible on that account so called was the result of the fancy and Caprice of the Editor.

Your letter has induced me to examine the subject and has led me to make (that which is at least to me) a Discovery, namely that from the time of the Reformation, the translators of the English Bible probably influenced by biggoted hatred to the Roman Catholics and by an equally biggoted reverence for Martin Luther, have made their translations not from the original Hebrew, nor from the Latin Bibles especially

197 Alfred Stevens (1817-1875) was the son of a Blandford decorator and joiner. In 1833 the Rector of Blandford enabled him to travel to Italy where he spent nine years studying. On his return to England he pursued a successful career, mainly in stone, bronze and metalwork. In 1856 he won the competition for the monument to the Duke of Wellington in St Paul's Cathedral, although he did not live to see it completed.

that which is termed the Vulgate, but they have word for word made their translation immediately from the German translation of Martin Luther and like the Chinese Painters have copied his errors. To prove this I have now open before me the large Folio of the *Biblia Hebraica* of B.A. Montanus (Edit: 1609) which is remarkable for having the most strictly literal Latin translation from the Hebrew that is supposed ever to have been made, each Hebrew word having the corresponding Latin word placed over it. Now Montanus's translation of the passage in question is *'Et Consuerunt folia ficus et fecerunt sibi cingulas'* the Hebrew for which is [word cannot be rendered, Ed.] Again I find in a beautiful copy of the Vulgate which I possess, the same translation *'Et Consuerunt folia ficus et fecerunt sibi Perizonata'*, the only difference being the affectation of employing a Greek instead of a Latin word. It is therefore quite evident that the English Translation in truth ought to be "And they sewed fig Leaves together and made themselves Girdles or Belts." And there is a common sense in this, for the first attempts at dress has constantly been observed amongst primitive nations to be Girdles or Zones made of leaves or Feathers &c.

But in the English Bibles, and I have before me Viz. that of London 1677, the Oxford 1772, and the Cambridge 1762, the translation with the exception of the breeches is "And they sewed Fig Leaves together and made themselves Aprons." Now in the Original there is more authority for the word Apron that there is for Breeches, and this led me to seek the source from which this error was derived, and upon examining Martin Luther's German Bible, I have found the very words *"und flocten feigenblatter zusammen und machten ihnen Schurtze"* "And they sewed fig leaves together and made themselves Aprons". The word is pronounced shirtze and I have got into great disgrace with my wife by having innocently said that I had no doubt that our word shirt was derived from the German *schurtze* which means an Apron, only that our shirt is composed of two Aprons it being a garment intended to serve as a covering behind as well as before. I must further observe that our English translators have in like manner made their translation of the New Testament, neither from the Greek nor the Latin, but from the German of Luther, and as proof, he uniformally translates the word *Denarius*, which so frequently occurs (as in the Parable of the Good Samaritan, - the Tribute money &c &c) he I say translates it *Groschen* which is a small German coin, and this word our translators have turned into Penny, which leads to very erroneous notions, for the *Denarius*, the tenth part of he *As* or *Pondus* of the Romans, and the first silver coin ever struck by them, was worth about 7¾d of our money and in the time of Christ one *Denarius* was sufficient to support a man even handsomely for a day, so that the two Pence in our Bibles given by the Good Samaritan amounted in reality to 1s. 3½d and was more than sufficient to amply supply the wounded man for more than two days. I must also remark that in the Greek Testament the word *Denarius* is adopted, and yet they might without much impropriety have employed the word *Drachma* for the attic *Drachma* so nearly resembled in weight the *Denarius* that the Greek Physicians when they came to Rome employed the *Denarius* to weigh their medicines in the place of their National Coin the Attic *Drachma* to which they had previously been accustomed. My Wife joins in kind regards to both of you with yours ever most truly
Charles Hatchett.

D-RAC/C/48. Letter from the Rev. J. Cooke, of Chettle & Blandford to the Rev. T. Rackett.

Blandford Feb. 10th 1836
My Dear Sir,
Yesterday I found this letter [the letter is written at the back of a printed form from the Treasurer of the Incorporated Society for the Propagation of the Gospel in Foreign Parts, endorsed in MS. "No return has been received for the above" and the sum of 0.12.0 from Charlton and 2.0.0. from Spettisbury has been filled in. Note by Editor.] from Mr. Markland. I know not how an Officer of a Voluntary Charity can demand a return from a Village Rector yet thus it apears from his forwarding a blank form – I thought you took with you the form originally sent that you might copy the essential part of it when making the payment 2.12.0. You will find he says no return has been received. In this case Ministers send out a Kings Letter in favor of a Society towds. which they had just notified their intention of withdrawing the Government contribution & they have now promised £10,000 to the London Missionary Society for West India purposes the same contemplated in above letter. I once collected upwards of £30 under the authority of a Kings letter – from their recent frequency & other circumstances (in Country Parishes at least) they will soon become of as little use as the old Briefs[198] – Amount 0.0.0.

Henry Knight wd. be very glad if you would send an order on Sampson for £20 to be paid to him on acct. S. says he will do this if you will give him permission – Mrs. Holloway late Thalia Pearce has come to Spety. to live bringing three children with her – Her Husband having deserted her to live with another woman – The eldest son is about 11 years of age – she requested me to write you for leave to place this son at Haywards school without payment, Henry Green as being in good circumstances had a bill sent in by H. for tuition – Green complained to me and said he never either had or would contribute a farthing – I said having Houses of his own, together with his business as a Mason & a Publican I cd. not call his one of the poor Parish Children. It wd. depend on the Trustees on your return – Mr. White of Charlton desired me when I wrote to thank you for a fish – The labourers of both parishes are indignant at not having Xmas Beef many of them have discontinued their attendance at Church & Mr. Amer now opens the Spety. Meeting House at Church Hours – Stroud never attends one – Yesterday Mr. Bastard pointedly remarked that he understood you were to return home in the month of Jany. Mrs. Quantock & Daur. are residing in Mrs. Smiths old House – I was invited to Luncheon between the hours of Service one Sunday and found the Ladies very chatty & Mamma inclined to be good to the poor – I have had £4 from Sampson for the Widows &c. Since your last letter I met with the followd. address in the newspapers Hebrew Review Office 17 – Milman St. Bedford

198 These were Letters patent issued by the Sovereign as Head of the Church, licensing a collection in Churches throughout England for a specified object. They became obsolete in practice in 1588. (HSLD). The date given by Dewar is erroneous: Briefs were abolished by Act of Parliament in 1828, although individual collections continued to be authorized by 'Royal Letter' for some years after this.

Row. I have written in pencil on the other side which you can rub out if you wish. With very kind regards to you all
I am very sincerely Yrs. J. Cooke.

Letter from J.B. Knight to Rev. T. Rackett[199].
West Lodge 3rd Dec. 1838
My dear Sir,
I send you a sketch of the stones on the barrow which Mr. & Mrs. Solly had not found when I was last at Spettisbury, as perhaps they may not yet have ascertained its position – It is where I conjectured it was, i.e., in the first arable field that you enter from Bere down in the direction of Roke down, and is 70 or eighty yards on your right after you are through the gate with your horse's head towards the west – It is not conspicuous as to heighth of the mound; but readily discoverable by the circumstance of an elder stunted bush, or bushes, growing on the top of it – There is another barrow south of it, & fronting you as you enter the gate, which on the south side shows the crown of a stone but this has been plowed over. (There are two pease ricks in the south west corner of the field which is a large one). I give these marks as they may not fail to find these barrows which I think must be curious when further developed – The stones are precisely like those of the Deverill Barrow but those that appear are buried almost to their surface; more no doubt are undiscovered as yet in both barrows. Your way will be to go up to Kingston – up Stonylands as if you were going to Whitchurch but turn to your left over Bere down to the end of Bere common cornfield when the Gate will be before you as you proceed in a S.W. direction., We all join in kind respects to yourself & Mr. & Mrs. Solly not forgetting Miss Thomasine. I shall be at Spettisbury on the apportionment[200] as soon as possible. Believe me to be, Dr. Sir,
Yours very sincerely
J.B. Knight.

199 This letter is not listed in the Dorset History Centre catalogue to the Rackett Papers and despite several searches in the collection, it has not been located. John Baverstock Knight (1785-1859) was a surveyor from Blandford who worked for several local landowners including the Farquharson family. He bought West Lodge, Piddletrenthide in 1812 and lived there until his death. He is better known today as a painter of local landscapes and portraits. He was an intimate friend of Rev.Thomas Rackett and spent many hours sketching with him.
200 He is referring to the tithe apportionment. Under the Tithe Commutation Act of 1836, tithes (a tenth of goods paid to the parson) which had traditionally been paid in kind, were commuted to monetary payments. The apportionment was drawn up to assess the liability of parishioners for payment, and was usually accompanied by a map of the parish showing where their land lay. Baverstock Knight is known to have been a Commissioner on local inclosure awards, and it is quite likely that he would have worked on tithe commutation as well.

D-RAC/K153C. Account of opening of Some Barrows on Roke Down, 1840, written a day or two after by me, D. Solly[201].

In a Barrow on Roke Farm, the property of J.S.E. Drax Esq. we observed a large stone weighing about a ton and a half under which was a deposit of burnt bones. The underside of the stone immediately in contact with this deposit was coloured as if by fire. In clearing away a little further, on the same level and about a foot from the deposit we discovered a bronze dagger[202] measuring in length with an ivory handle, the blade beautifully grooved and the whole exquisitely polished; a small guard also of ivory was fixed to the top of the blade with bronze studs, and a small spear or arrow head of the same material was laid close to the former. The deposit was on the south side of the barrow at about one third of its height from the level of the ground. A section was then made through the centre of the barrow which was a very large one measuring in diameter and in height. Exactly under the highest part on the floor of the barrow the workmen struck upon some bones which proved to be two skeletons doubled up and pressed into a very large urn which had been inverted over them but had been broken probably by the weight of the earth at the time of the deposit. There was a slight basin like hollow in the chalk under the urn but no articles whatever in it or near it. This may be considered as the primary interment. We heard that on a former occasion three urns had been taken out of the same barrow on the east side, one of which contained some glass beads.

Another barrow was then opened on the Down to the north by sinking a shaft to the centre. The middle part was of chalk rubble surrounded by brown earth. Half way down we came to an arch of flints among which on the north side was a piece of sandstone of the size of an half peck loaf, under which was found a small circle of black earth and charcoal; a little lower, stones of the same kind were found on the other three points and also in the middle, immediately under which was a skeleton lying on its side with the legs gathered up, which according to E. King Esq. in his *Munimenta Antiqua* is the primitive form of burial. The head was to the north and the teeth very beautiful. A few small splinters of wood were found on one side which led to the supposition that a spear or arrow might have been placed there but none were discovered. As this skeleton was a little raised from the floor of the barrow, it was removed and the earth cleared away to the chalk but nothing was found beneath.

The most curious of the tumuli in that neighbourhood is one a few yards distant from the one described. It has been opened at different times but from what we could gather from those who remembered the opening of it its construction was as follows. A cist 4 feet in diameter was made in the chalk round which were placed several stones and another laid over the top. There urns we were told had been found under the stone but hearing that the cist had not yet been explored to the bottom we

201 See *Proceedings* of Dorset Natural History and Archaeological Society, Vo. 90, 1968, for an article on *Rev Thomas Rackett of Spetisbury and the 'Barrow Diggers'* by H.S.L. Dewar.

202 The bronze dagger was subsequently lost in a fire at the Solly's house in Poole. (HSLD)

cleared it out but found only a fragment of pottery. A Barrow to the was pointed out as having been partially opened and three urns taken out very near the top.

D-RAC/D/ 78. Letter from Mrs. M. Blunt to Rev & Mrs. Rackett.

Enham House,
March 17th.
Many thanks to you my dear Mr. & Mrs. Rackett for your very interesting & most welcome joint letter – You cannot give us more pleasure than by indulging us in this way whenever health and time will permit – my object in writing now, is, that Mr. Caley may be informed that in addition to the seals he wished to see at Col. Iremongers, when I dined there a few days ago, he told me there was a thick Book attached to the Title deeds containing he believed the history of the Convent[203] which he should be very glad to have a translation of – it must be I suppose a very valuable record, and particularly so to Mr. C. who I think you said was engaged in a work describing old Monasteries[204], at all events you could get at a knowledge of its contents which Col. I. would be glad to do – and will have much pleasure in shewing everything belonging to Wherwell Priory to any friends to whom as lovers of Antiquity it would be interesting – do you know the inscription on Pompey's pillar? – The translation of that Col. I wishes to have – he has the original – amongst some of the learned in Dorset, Lincolnshire or London, I ventured to give him hopes I could succeed – we have laughed over your friend Waterton and her Wanderings most heartily. Travellers are priveledged persons, and we cannot contradict them if they do tell marvellous stories but the crocodiles feet being twisted to form a bridle – and the snake stories are rather difficult to follow – I have heard of a profession in Town the Wonder Makers, who get capital pay by writing for the newspapers – with such a happy talent as Mr. W. possesses what fortunes they would make. Denham & Clappertons Quarto[205] you would not find hang heavy on hand as Mr. Southey's[206] must do – we have been more interested & amused by their travels than any book we have read for some time past & are anxious to follow up the track they have taken – the people are such a superior race of beings to any, one had an idea could exist in the midst of a desert – I am happy to tell you that our Kitchen Garden has fared much better than our neighbours in general – Peas are looking very lively – beans coming up – we have not been reduced at any time to Potatoes – I have a fresh cargo of plants for the Greenhouse & garden coming to day & shall be very busy to the end of April when we look forward to seeing

203 The reference is to the Benedictine Nunnery of Wherwell, 3½ miles SSE. of Andover, Hants. This was founded by Elfrida, widow of King Edgar, given to the first Lord Delawarr at the dissolution, and passed to the Iremonger family. (HSLD)

204 John Caley (1760-1834), archivist and antiquary, prepared a new edition of Dugdale's *Monasticon* which appeared in six volumes between 1817 and 1830.

205 *Narrative of Travels and discoveries in Northern and Central Africa, by* Major D. Denham, Capt. H. Clapperton and Dr. Oudney, 1826.

206 Robert Southey (1774-1843) poet.

all our friends in Town. It is to be hoped that the stormy winds will abate before our baggagers by steam set off for Scotland which they propose doing either the end of the month or the beginning of April, and they rather hope to enlist Mr. G. Harris to be of their party – Edward & Jim will then make some pleasant excursions together while Shirley remains with her Father – I had no idea of the Sollys spending the winter in Lincolnshire; with their various pursuits & intercourse with their Scientific and musical friends, No doubt time has passed very pleasantly – they will join you in Town e'er long I conclude – what do you think of the mine of Etruscan Vases discovered in Tuscany & placed in the Museum at Florence 800 in number all of the greatest beauty in form &c.? (Po)mpei treasures &c. how can we resist a visit to Italy? I am very glad Mr. Miles has met with a little pleasant assistance which I hope will lead to a permanent provision – his exertions deserve encouragement and reward – the young Artist Catterson Smith[207] who took our likeness at Kensington in Chalks, we advised to come down to Andover & we would do all we could to recommend him – he arrived the 10th Janry. and has been ever since most successfully employed by all the neighbourhood round, and does not know when he shall be at liberty again to return to Town – he talks of going to Salisbury & I have no doubt will succeed anywhere – 15' tempts so many people to sit for their Picture who would not like to give a higher price – his style is improved too by this constant practice – I was at Wallop yesterday where he has been very happy in getting a speaking likeness of James - & is to do the young people next week – my Nephew Edw. Powlett having finished his studies at Oxford is now Mr. Harris's travelling Companion on the Circuit which finishes at Dover - & he talks of taking him to France for a fortnight – which would be a grand treat – to return to the subject of Gardening which is uppermost in my thoughts just now – I had another No. of the Horticultural Transactions lent me lately, in which there were some very useful hints – one for a Pit for preserving vegetables thro' the winter from frost merely made in a rough way without any expence in wood – another for cultivating plants in moss which latter I am trying – I assure you my greenhouse plants are quite beautiful – such fine health and such a show of bloom coming out – I do not know how I shall bear to leave them – I intended Mama to have reported well of herself – but she leaves me to do this of her – to day – she gets out airing constantly and is surprisingly recovered – not overstrong yet – we wish dear Mrs. Rackett could give as good an account of herself – our love and every good wish attends you from all our circle to Mr. & Mrs. R. & believe me, Yours very sincerely,
M. Blunt.

Mrs. Burrough & her niece Miss B. called here on Thursday – she is come to stay till the Judge finishes his Circuit – is quite well – Mrs. Best expecting an increase very shortly – Fenwicks settled at Gibraltar and tolerably comfortable – poor old Mr. Burrough has had two falls – but is much better than one could expect.

207 Stephen Catterson Smith (1806-1872), English portrait painter.

D-RAC/E/104. Letter from Mrs. St. Barbe, & C. St. Barbe Junr., & Mrs. E. Pulteney. Posted at Lymington.

My dear Mrs. Rackett,
As Dorothea would tell you how very unwell I was on Monday, you will not be much surprised to hear that I have not made great advances towards amendment by this time; I am seldom free from the shortness of breath, excepting at night; the medical I usually employ is in London, so that I do not make any change in my medicine until his return, which will be I believe tomorrow –

Will you tell our aged friend Mrs. Farquharson that I feel very anxious to learn she is better. [Interlined here by another hand are the words, "and I also join the same sentiment". Ed]. I regret that I did not desire Mrs. Grane to write me on Monday or Tuesday; I do not trouble her with a letter just now, as I know you can any day communicate intelligence of me to Blandford, & I trust a few days hence I shall be able to give a better report of myself. – The autographs were received as originals: soon after they were exhibited, Edward came in & Cowper was handed to him as a delicious morsel by Mr. Charles the Antiquarian. I hope you are satisfied with the success of the deception; perhaps some superstitious people would say I was suffering for plotting against my husband; ill as I was I rather enjoyed the sport.

It will be most prudent to give up the pen to those who are better able to use it than I am at present, but I must first beg my dear friends at Spettisbury to accept my affectionate regards,
Believe me my dear Mrs. Rackett,
Your sincere obliged
M. St. Barbe.
Wednesday Evening.

On my return home I opened the packet of autographs you kindly sent me, and they are indeed a great acquisition. On a second examination of Cowpers (I had risen rather earlier than usual that day) I discovered the writing was rather too fresh considering the writer had been dead several years – therefore I am inclined to think that it was cooked up to impose upon you by some witty friend – however the verses contain most excellent advice, and I hope they will not be forgotten by me. – If you wish to refer to the View of Ringwood Church &c. in *Gent. Mag.* It is in the Vol. for 1807. – (Nov?)
Adieu my Dear Sir, Yrs. Most truly.
C. St. B. Junr.

I was much mortified that I could not venture to give my dear Friend the meeting at Ringwood – I had not been out in the carriage for many days, having found that my cough was always increased by an airing: I believe it would have been better for poor Mary that I had gone instead of her little Prattlers, who I feared would be oppressive to her. She was much fatigued, & the next day very hysterical, & I fear it (will) take her some days to recover it [sic].

I can assure my dear Dorothea that she is not forgotten here by her friends & acquaintances, & as a proof of their taste, they do not take a fancy to every stranger. We have had two Beauties here for many weeks; they display'd everything behind and before, above and below that they thought could excite admiration, threw themselves into studied attitudes, which thro' their thin draperies shewed the full form of their beauteous Limbs. They were lively too, & even witty, but what was the consequence? After they had gone thro' a course of Balls with which it was thought a duty to treat them, all the Town, young and old, - Male & Female, rejoiced when they were gone! It brought to my recolllection some lines I heard when I was young

"There is no woman where there's no reserve
And 'tis on plenty your poor Lovers Starve".

Adieu my beloved Friends.
E. Pulteney.

D-RAC/D/78. The Chelsea Pensioner's receipt for Gout or Rheumatism, sent by Mrs. M. Blount to Mrs. T. Rackett

Honey clarified 2lbs. till reduced to 1 lb.
1 Drachm of Guaicum in powder
2ozs. of Flower of Sulphur
1¼ oz. Rhubarb in powder
1 oz. Cream of Tartar
1 Nutmeg grated
¼ lbs. of ginger powdered.
Mixed well together. Two tea spoons full to be taken in warm liquid every night at Bedtime for ten days. To be taken again at intervals.
Entered in a book.

D-RAC/D/78. Letter from Mrs. Blunt to Mrs. Rackett
[Perhaps written from Wallop. Ed.]

My still dear Friend
Though you and I seem to have cut off all written intercourse; it may be we may ken one another when we chance to meet, either in this world, or the next. – The winter has I guess put you out of sorts, as it has done your old friend – and even much stouter folks. – but we are patching up, and propping up the old Vehicle, to try to set it agoing once more; & as the experiment cannot be made, of its good plight, under a journey of 67 miles, and it will go, if it can go at all, on 13th or 14th April. 'Tis probable you may be in your Town house – where if you do not labour too much for your strength you may have a great many pleasant drives, & chats with your Relatives.

Harriet has engaged to protect 3 nieces who are to be our inmates at Kensington; not for gaiety; but for improvement. Masters do not abound upon the Salisbury Plains; & as Education is the order of the day, there is no doing without them.

I think it right to tell you not to trust money in Country Banks – the Cash we have had in the failure of Wakeford's at Andover has been a 2nd deluge in the Country all around: - the number whom it has involved are past counting.

You see Sr. C. Blunt of Heathfield Park[208] has had a Son & Heir? – My dear old Lady B. was so anxious that it should be so, that for the honour of our Sex, I am glad a female did not come instead – as she was undesired, she wd. not have been welcome. Your good Man & the Sollys are well I hope? – If when you are in the cue you would send me a short sealed note to Phillimore Place Lofts will send it in my parcel – the shortness of the note may tempt you once more to write to
Yrs. affectly.
M. Blunt.

D-RAC/C/74. [No date] Letter from Mary C. Forth to the Rev. Thomas Rackett. From Denham Place, Nr. Uxbridge.

Dear Sir,
So many years have elapsed since we met, that I fear I should have some chance of your forgetting me even by name did I not recall yourself to your remembrance through the medium of my much valued and lamented friend and guardian Mr. Lane. I have a sister Sir, who has for some time given her attention to drawing in the botanical style hand her performances have met with the approbation of a great many Botanical Gardeners who approve her flowers and say if she could procure the patronage of a man of taste and science known in the great world, they do not doubt of her success. I took the liberty of naming you and the reply was "we could not hope for a better patron."

Dr. Symms was likewise named to whom I believe you are personally known – my sister will wait on you any day, and hour you may appoint with specimens of her performances. An artist suggested likewise: as Botany was so much the fashion that a Botanical Drawing School might answer. I am now in a family in which I have resided 14 years – should my sister succeed in forming an Establishment of the kind I have mentioned, it would be the means of uniting us in a comfortable Home in our latter days – I must apologize Sir for intruding on your valuable time; but the recollection of your benevolence and readiness to oblige persuaded me that the liberty that I have taken will be pardoned. Hoping that you and your family are well, I have the honour to be
Your most respectful & obedient,
Mary Catherine Forth.

208 Sir Charles Blunt (1775-1840), M.P. for Lewes.

D-RAC/C/61. Letter from W.A. Miles to Rev. T. Rackett.

Oak Inn
Milbourne St Andrews
Saturday
Sir, I am now at the above address for a day or two, in order to pack my Urns for removal, having left that vile & wretched hole of Wareham – I intend getting away from here as soon as possible as tavern Bills are pleasanter to incur than pay, if therefore Monday will be a convenient day for your coming over here, I shall be delighted in exhibiting to you such fine specimens of ancient Urns – and under the hope of seeing you, I will not actually commence packing them until after 12 o'clock on Monday Morning. With compliments to the Ladies, I have the honour to remain
Your obedt. Humble Servt.
Will. Aug. Miles

P.S./Over
P.S.
I returned your books & I hope they arrived safe – and you will forgive the rude manner, but I was so hurried in packing up that I really had not time to express how sincerely I felt obliged for your kindness. If Mrs. White would wish to see the urns I should be happy in having this present opportunity of showing them.

[Note: the above letter is endorsed at the back with the words "Mr. Miles about the Barrow – Milbourne, probably in Rackett's writing. Ed.]

D-RAC/E/104. Letter from Mrs. Pulteney to ? Mrs. Rackett. [No address]

You have as I expected discovered my meaning, but your imagination has on this occasion, been rather too excursive (an error very pardonable in *Belle-esprits* & persons of genius) it has carried you beyond the limits of my plan which is simply a new system of orthography; and will not, I apprehend, immediately affect the general politics of Europe, great as is the influence of this Republic may be over that as well as every other science. Your panegyrics dear Madame would at another time be oppressive to my modesty, as somewhat exceeding my [any?] merit that I have hitherto acquired, but for the present, let that quality be suffered to sleep; for, warmed as I am with the great object I have in view, I must like other great personages (Ovid for instance) be indulged in overstepping, a little, the bounds of common modesty, by predicting my own immortality, when this system of mine shall be universally adopted (as doubtless it will) & all its advantages fully comprehended, my name shall flourish, and be had in honour when that of the petty, paltry Dumouriez[209] has been long lost in oblivion; I beg

209 Charles Francois Dumouriez (1739-1823) deserted the French Army during the Revolution and became a royalist intriguer.

leave however to decline the task you have allotted me: of compelling him to relinquish his conquests – I should think I was acting like Canute, when he commanded the sea to go back. You see Madam, I scorn to use any but great comparisons. – Inclosed you will find a small specimen of my new system of orthography by which you will be enabled to comprehend, and to assist me in my undertaking, for it cannot be supposed that a work of this magnitude can be completed by one person – all I shall contend for is the honour of the invention. You will see Madame that I mean to relieve these harassed Republicans, particularly five of them whose burthens are greater than the rest by employing as few of them as possible in their daily tasks, for a total abolition of their slavery I fear must not be attempted, at least till the world has become more enlightened & a shorter road to knowledge is discovered – I am for doing things in a gentle & progressive manner; not like Paine[210] & Dumouriez, overturning the world at once, in order to mend its condition. Nor will I like most Patriots, pretend to loose all private interests in that of the public – I honestly confess my regret, that the learned of the present age, - this Nation, & my Husband in particular, will reap but little benefit from my scheme, as it will scarcely answer the expence to have his present library new printed, his shelves therefore, as well as those of others, must continue to groan under the weight of an useless load of letters, paper and leather. It is for Posterity then that I labour, & Posterity will undoubtedly be grateful for the inestimable advantages it will enjoy.

Adieu! Dear Madame,
Believe me ever your obliged
hum. Servt.

D-RAC/C/74. Letter from Maria Lister to Rev. Thomas Rackett, undated but possibly 1839[211]

My dear Sir
I fear the dullness of this autumn season will give me no means of interesting you as for chemical news you will have already heard from my Uncle that Faraday[212] has at length obtained the spark from the electric eel. My Brother was so pleased that he talked of little else for a week. The business of moving the treasures of the Museum from the

210 Thomas Paine (1737-1809), political reactionary and author of *The Rights of Man* (1791).
211 She lived at 8 Lincoln's Inn Fields, London. She was probably the daughter of Dr William Lister (1756-1830), physician and Governor of St Thomas's Hospital, who lived at that address. His wife was Elizabeth Solly, a cousin of Dorothea's husband Samuel. Details of another letter from Miss Lister to Mary Anning can be found in *Proceedings* of the Dorset Natural History and Archaeological Society, Vol. 71, Pp. 184-8
212 Michael Faraday (1791-1867). He was assistant to Sir Humphrey Davy at the Royal Institution and conducted pioneering experiments into chemistry and electricity, later becoming its first Fullerian Professor. In 1839 he produced his theory of electrical action based on his many years of experimentation. That same year his health broke down and he did not resume work until the mid-1840s.

old part into the north wing[213] is going on very rapidly & I imagine it involves a new arrangement of the geological specimens for those in the side cases are yours. I wanted my American Brother to compare the Lyme fossils with those he is accustomed to see. He has a good collection both of fossil and recent shells no less than 50 from this river alone and had promised to bring some but the long land journey he had to take when much luggage is an encumbrance, deterred him. Geology according to him is a patronized science in the United States. There is a salaried appointment of Geologist in every state his business is to study the nature of the stratifications & lay reports from time to time as he proceeds with his labours before the Governor. There are going to be excavations made about Dover[214] in connection with some railroad which it is expected it will bring to light many Roman memorials. The Antiquarian must rejoice at these modern improvements however much the lover of the picturesque will regret the way in which all the most beautiful hills are to be levelled or tunnelled. I am sorry not to have heard of your having made some excursion this autumn & half hoped that you might have made Lyme & had some news of poor Miss Anning[215]. I have not heard from or of her since August. Have you had your Skipper? Mama & all our circle beg their kindest remembrances.
Believe me with much respect
Yours truly obliged
Maria Lister

D-RAC/E/126. Letter from Mary Anning to Dorothea Solly[216]

Lyme, June 10 1844
Dear Madam
be pleased to accept my most Grateful thanks; for your still condesending to remember me, as also for yr most interesting account of the lectures (Lyme being such an out of way Town, that I seldom get any scientific news Miss's Phillpots[217] desires their kind Compts and were so delighted with the information contained in yr letter; that they fingred it to copy; so I can only remark on it generally as truly believing from what little I have seen of the fossil World and Natural History, I think the connection or analogy between the Creatures of the former, and present World excepting as to size, is much greater than is generally supposed, as we have not had either storms or

213 Work began on Sir Robert Smirke's new building for the British Museum in 1823 and finished in 1853. Collections were moved in as each of the four wings was finished.

214 Dover's first railway station was opened in 1844 by the South Eastern Railway but construction of the line took several years due to the difficult nature of the terrain.

215 Mary Anning was struggling financially in the 1830s. In the last years of her life she suffered from ill health, dying of cancer in 1847.

216 This letter is discussed in *Proceedings* of Dorset Natural History and Archaeological Society, Vol. 74, Pp. 175-7

217 Elizabeth Philpot (1780-1857), amateur fossil collector and palaeontologist who collaborated with Mary Anning in her discoveries. She lived in Lyme with her sisters Louise and Margaret.

Landslips this last winter, there has been but little found, but hope still Mr Solly will be tempted down during Miss Solly's holidays, I did not think that Miss S. would have remembred me, am truly glad to hear so good an account of her health, as also to hear a mended account of Miss Lister; should the latter lady condsend to remember pray give my best and respectful remembrances to her, Dr Knight left Lyme a year and half since for Dorchester and about 6 months since he buried his wife and I have not heared of him since - if we have not had a Landslip we have had a tremendious fire skip viz. 52 houses including 3 inns it began at the George Inn commonly called Monmouth house, the wind being very high, the second house Sellers in in broad street and cleared all that side as far as the bridge close by were you lodged skipped over yr old Lodgings and then burnt both sides of the street viz. namely Comb Street, to cut off the fire in broad street they pulled down they shambles I do regret the Old Clock that had stood for Centries I am glad you have made the aquaintance of my Old friend Sir. H. De la Beach[218], I will not longer trespass on yr valuable time with best and respectful remembrances to Mr and Miss Solly and also to yourself.
I remain dear Madam
Your greatly Obliged Servant
Mary Anning
Addressed to Mrs Solly, 48 Upper Gower Street, Bedford Square, London.

D-RAC/K/157B. Verse on the Lord High Chancellor of Great Britain, Eldon of Encombe, by T. Rackett. 1819

On downy pillow rests his Pate
And soon forgets his cares of State
On Purbeck downs recruits his health
And quite forgets to spend his wealth.

D-RAC/K/157B. Verse to David Garrick Esq., by T. Rackett. ?c. 1772

For thy late favors how shall I reveal
My inward sentiments or what I feel
My week abilities can boast no art
To praise thy Bounteous Hand I now aspire
How weak my Pow'r how ardent my desire
As nature spoke tis said by Shakespeare's pen
To charm the Amaz'd Astonish'd sons of men
E'en so when thou by Heaven & Shakespeare fir'd

218 Sir Henry de la Beche (1796-1855), the first Director of the Geological Survey of Great Britain and first President of the Palaeontographical Society. He was a lifelong friend, mentor and financial supporter of Mary Anning.

To tell his name & speak his work aspir'd
His pow'rful strokes thy matchless force impress'd
And unresisted passion stormed the breast
The Poet's merit too in thee we see
What Shakespeare was what Shakespeare wish'd to be
But why should I endeavour to Display
Thy wond'rous worth in this my first Essay.

D-RAC/K/157B. Verse by T. Rackett.

Turn'd out of my House, Goods and chattels removing
All my Pictures ta'en down! - what with lifting & shoving
I got a sad bruise, and a scratch and a gore
On this side and that both behind and before
'Tis no wonder from bottom to top I was sore?
But a medical Friend who perceived my disaster,
Has set me to rights, by the gift of a Plaister.
When I am favour'd with a Call
You'll see the fact and proof of all
That strictly true's each word I say
-Nor is the Plaister cast away.
T.R.

D-RAC/K/157B. Verse, said to be by the Earl of Ilchester. Copied by Rev. T. Rackett.

To be written on Four Termini, describing the Boundaries of a Churchyard

We trace the limits of man's last retreat,
Where good & bad, where poor lie mixed with great
Each with his share of sin but each alone
For mercy trusting to th' Almighty Throne

In this small space is mad Ambition laid
Who for itself alone thought earth was made;
Pride from her pinnacle thus low is tost,
Here ev'ry hope of Vanity is lost;
To this coarse bed is Luxury confin'd
And Av'rice leaves her darling heaps behind.

Yet think not we encompass Vice alone,
Virtues transcendent to their rest are gone.
Bosoms that melted at each tale of woe,

And Hearts forgiving of their greatest foe:

Hands open to each charitable deed,
And doubly bounteous when the claim was need.
Then heedless wand'rer, stay thy steps and learn
To place in Virtue's path thy great concern;
Tho' all unwarned alike, come here to lie,
The Man who best has lived, knows best to die.

D-RAC/K/157A. [another draft is in K/157B] Lines presumed by Rev. T. Rackett to have been written by his grandmother on Mr. [Charles?] Hatchett's marriage with Miss Collick[219].

1
Cupid rose at dawn of day
As Venus once desir'd
She bid him Dorsetshire survey
Where sporting youths retired

2
He lightly tripp'd it o'er the plain
No footsteps could he trace
From hill to hill he skip'd again
And strolled from place to place

3
No human form could he espy
Nor any sound could hear
Till feather'd songsters round him fly
And bleating flocks appear

4
But now a voice did him surprize
With Notes most sad and sweet
It was a drooping Partridge cryes
A suppliant at his feet.

5
My tender wife and children dear
On yonder down they lie
'Tis for their safety that I fear
Who scarce are fledged to fly

6
Think on the danger they must run
Perhaps on this dread day
From Hatchetts never failing Gun

219 Charles Hatchett married Elizabeth Martha Collick (1756-1837) at St Martin-in-the-Fields on 24 March 1786.

No bird can fly away.

7

My brother once for flight so fam'd
Swift as the lark he fled
But at that Brother Hatchett aim'd
And shot him thro' the HEAD.

8

While thus he spake sighs heav'd his breast
Dear Cupid take our part
Revenge our race and give us rest
Pierce Hatchett thro' the Heart.

9

Reflecting on his tender grief
And touch'd by Mercy's plea
Cupid replied for your relief
You may depend on me.

10

A maid by nature form'd to please
Would Reynold's perfection trace,
He'd draw her elegance and ease
To yr. graces she'd add grace

11

Music she knows and plays with stile
That so enchants the ear
Love listens from Olimpia's Hill
Well pleased her notes to hear.

12

Apollo once came down in haste
Apollo loves a frolick
From every muse he stole their taste
And gave it all to Collick.

13

On this sweet bird you may rely
Tho' he may aim at you
This nymph is present to his eye
Sole object of his view

14

The Bird with pleasure did Depart
Rejoycing took his flight
Nor did young Cupid's feeling heart
Experience less delight.

D-RAC/K/157B. Verse by 'Maria', written from Brighton, probably sent to Thomas Rackett. [No date]

POUR PRENDRE CONGE
In vain for three seasons each art has been tried
I am still unwed and unwed must abide;
In vain have my Mother and I every night,
Tried to gudgeon the Men, but the Flats[220] will not bite;
Sad, sad is my fate, every scheme has miscarried,
I was twenty last Christmas, and still am Unmarried.
In vain to our dinners were dozens invited,
And scores with our parties at night were delighted;
Ah! Was it for this that I sang till my throat
Grew so hoarse, not an ear could distinguish a note,
(Though of course every hearer pronounc'd it Divine,
That the words were so charming, the Music so fine!)
Oh! Was it for this that I danced each quadrille,
With a fairy like grace and a Paris taught skill?
That I lost all my roses by keeping late hours
Till now I must cull some from Ackerman's bowers.
Oh! Horrid! three months dear Sir Thomas I thought
In my snares a rich treasure at last had been caught;
Every morning his Tilbury whisk'd me along,
In the evening he sought me all other among;
My partner when dancing, companion when still,
The page at my back, and the slave of my will,
To carry my fan how happy was he!
How delighted he seemed when he sweeten'd my tea!
When I sung, with what ardour enraptur'd he listen'd,
When I smiled, what delight in his eyes ever glisten'd!
Oh! Sir Thomas, Sir Thomas, may grief be my lot
For the whole of next winter, if thou art forgot!
Mama too, dear creature, how kindly she plann'd
Fresh Schemes to entice to propose for my hand!
To day 'twas a dinner – her Dishes were eat up;
Tomorrow a rout – the best she could get up;
The dinner was eat, and the rout it was over,
But alas! not an offer was made by my Lover!
Every ball in the county was graced by our faces
Corporation, Election, Assizes and Races!

220 Students of slang will be interested in the growth of a 'flat' into a 'square' in about 150 years. (HSLD) In 1965, at the height of the 'swinging sixties', it was fashionable to refer to those not following the latest trends (particularly the older generation) as 'square'. As Dewar noted, fashions in slang change, and the term has since declined in popular use.

What money was spent at the Play house, where often
I fancied fair Juliet my lover might soften;
And that fiction might help to promote declaration
But alas! all on earth is but grief and vexation;
After all our endeavours, and plots, and advances
Routs, dinners, wines, dishes, songs music, and dances
One morn on returning from Calls, unexpected
His card on the table I found, but connected
Three grief speaking letters – two 'P's. & a C
Reared their forms as in mockery of love & of me.
Maria

D-RAC/K/154C. Account of some Greek coins found in Dorsetshire, by the Rev. Thos. Rackett, F.S.A., in a letter to Henry Ellis Esq.[221] This draft copy in Rackett's script is marked "Read June 7 1832"[222]

Dear Sir,
An inhabitant of the parish of Charlton Marshall in Dorsetshire having brought to me some Greek coins which he found in a field that had been ploughed from time immemorial but was for the first time parcelled out in small allotments for the cultivation of potatoes, I directed him to make enquiry and procure whatever coins he could meet with under similar circumstances in the same place or elsewhere. And by assiduity in the research among labourers and other, I have in the course of six months been enabled to collect upwards of an hundred coins of the Kings of Syria Macedon, Bythinia, Syrmium & Egypt, & of the States & colonies of Antioch Carthage, Cos, Mamertini Rhegium Syracuse Neapolis &c., of which a list is subjoined from various places remote from any habitation, others where vestiges of ancient population are very evident. The coins from Abbey Milton were found a few years ago by a person who discovered at the same time a gold Torques intrinsically worth £30, of which the late Lady Caroline Damer became possessed.

About 35 Roman Coins of Various Emperors from Augustus to Gratian some

221 Henry Ellis (1777-1869), one of two assistants at the Bodleian Library, and subsequently assistant-keeper of books and manuscripts at the British Museum. He was appointed Principal Keeper in 1827. He was a fellow of the Society of Antiquaries and acted as their Secretary for forty years.

222 Several drafts of this letter exist, showing slight variations. They reveal something of the care with which Rackett prepared his material for learned Societies, amending and re-drafting until he was satisfied with the result. One variant has been published in part by J.G. Milne in *Finds of Greek Coins in the British Isles.* O.U.P. 1948, pp. 18-19. It is of interest to note that the gold 'Torques' belonging to Lady Caroline Damer, mentioned by Rackett in this communication was published in *Antiquity*, Vol. XXXVI, No. 146, June 1963, by Dr John Coles, F.S.A. and subsequently sold at auction by Sotheby's in 1964, the purchaser being the Birmingham City Museum and Art Gallery. (HSLD) This paper is not listed in the Dorset History Centre catalogue to the Rackett Papers and despite several searches in the collection, it has not been located.

Nuremberg counters a penny of Edw. I & sixpence of Queen Elizabeth were brought in the course of the enquiries.

It may be proper to add that some years ago between 70 & 80 silver coins similar to those in Borlases *Cornwall*[223] were discovered at Okeford Fitzpaine, & a silver coin figured in Gough's *Camden*[224]. No. 47 was found last year at Langton. I have considered the fact of finding a number of Carthaginian Greek & Syracusan coins of sufficient importance to be communicated to the Society.

That a commercial intercourse subsisted between the Britons & the Inhabitants of the East in very remote times appears from the glass beads and gold ornaments found in Barrows, where no coins or iron weapons have been discovered. And various circumstances seem to favour the supposition that a colony was formed in this part of the Island.

The name of the Inhabitants of Dorsetshire Durotriges Dourotriges Ptolemy from *Dou* – water & *trig* an inhabitant or the British name *Dwr Gweir* literally Sea Men is precisely the appelation which would be given to Strangers who came by sea which appeared to be their element (as the term *Nordmanni* was applied to Men who came from the North) and who formed a settlement in the Country.

Camden indeed interprets the name as men inhabiting the Sea shore, but this term would equally suit the Damnonii of Devonshire, the Belgae of Hampshire or all the inhabitants of the Southern coast. It would only apply to those in the vicinity of the coast and could not designate those who live on the confines of Wiltshire & Somersetshire Upwards of thirty miles distant from it.

In addition to this we may observe that there are a number of earthworks still remaining in various parts of the county too regular and artificial to be the work of those whom we call the Aboriginal Britons whose Camps villages trackways & boundaries are irregular & easily distinguishable nor do they appear to be Roman by pavements or other indications relating to that people. Of these some remarkable ones occur in the Isle of Purbeck, at Charlton, between Bere and Milbourne and at Poorstock to which may be added the Labyrinth[225] formerly existing at Pimperne and another at Yateminster.

I have considered the fact of finding a number of Carthaginian Greek & Syracusan coins the date of some of them viz of Seleucus, Philip II & Alexander the Great being upwards of 300 years before the Christian era of sufficient importance to be communicated to the Society as it appears to afford very decisive evidence of an intercourse these people [sic] respectively with Britain. It will serve to strengthen & in some instances perhaps confirm the accounts of ancient navigators Pithias & others who from their deficiency in Geographical accuracy have been too much discredited. The circumstances of meeting with coins of Carthage & of Prusias King of Bythinia

223 William Borlase (1696-1772), rector of Ludgvan and author of *The Antiquities of Cornwall* (1754) and *The Natural History of Cornwall* (1758).

224 Richard Gough published a major new edition of William Camden's *Britannia* in 1789.

225 The Labyrinth or Maze at Pimperne has been ploughed out, but there are remains of the Maze at Leigh in Yetminster.

9 Drawing of a Cromlech at Portesham by Thomas Rackett
(Hutchins, History of Dorset, *2nd edition, vol. ii, p. 310)*

the friend and ally of Hannibal will render the Northern expedition of Himilco[226] not so improbable as it has sometimes been considered and when we find a number of Syracusan Coins among which are two of Hiero[227] it affords a strong argument in favour of the original text of [illegible word here. Ed.] Athenaeus who, relating from Moschion the description of Hiero's ship[228] observes that the mainmast was procured *en tois oresin tes Brettanies.* Casaubon in a note on this passage has substituted [word illegible here. Ed.] merely because he thinks Britain was almost unknown to the Greeks. His words are Britannia *nomen in posteriere membro satin' ex fide? Mihi non Videtur qui sciam insulam iis temporibus Graecis Latinisque parum* [illegible word here. Ed.] *notam, Navigationem vero in Oceano oppido paucir adhuc tenatam. Legendum censeo en tois oresin tes Brettias in montibus Brutiorum eam partiae Italiae sic Graeci nominant.*

226 Himilco (fl. 5th century B.C.), sometimes referred to as Himilco the Navigator, was a Carthaginian sailor who sailed north along the Atlantic coast as far as the British Isles.
227 Hiero II was the Greek ruler of Syracuse from 270-215 B.C. He fought in the inconclusive First Punic War, after which he entered into a treaty with the Romans.
228 Athenaeus states (Loeb. Athenaeus V. 208) that "The ship was named Syracusia but when Hieron sent her forth – he changed the name to Alexandria". (HSLD)

It may here be not irrelevant to observe that the doubts of commentators are not always to be implicitly relied on. The accuracy of Herodotus which has been questioned has been confirmed in various instances by the observations of modern travellers. The use of Seals by the Saxons was formerly doubted by learned antiquaries but recent discoveries have established the practice beyond all controversy.

GENERAL INDEX

Places are indexed under their historic county.

www.ingramcontent.com/pod-product-compliance
Lightning Source LLC
Chambersburg PA
CBHW081138300726
48982CB00006B/1000
9780900339240